Where Will We

Go From Here?

2018 and beyond

Other Works by the Same Author

Books

Numberland
Bird
Quiet Answers
Three Gifts: The Eras of Science, Medicine, Religion
The Golden Prayer Puzzle
The Golden Prayer Search

Musical plays

Life Adds up in Numberland, the Musical
Musicland

Music and dialogue recordings

Numberland
Numberland Music
Musicland
Children's Musicland
Something Bright and Beautiful
Bird
Lessons from Bird

Where Will
We Go From Here?

2018 and beyond

By

Auriel Wyndham Livezey

Mountaintop Publishing

Published in the United States of America

Printed in the United States of America and abroad

ISBN 978-1-893930-13-1

Mountaintop Publishing, California

www.MountaintopPublishing.com

CONTENTS

Dear thinkers of the world
With kind, expansive view,
Please do note this book is
Written, especially for you!

Where Will We Go from Here?

2018 and beyond

Introduction

"Out of the blue"

Just when we thought 1968 had comfortably settled into the pages of history, 2018 came along fifty years later and completely changed that perception.

These two years appear to be twins. If not identical, they are certainly fraternal twins. Something momentous is obviously taking place. A new era was ushered in with 1968, and it seems that 2018 is accomplishing the same feat. If another new era is emerging, what will it be like? And where will it lead us in the future?

History repeats itself. That statement may be traced back hundreds of years, so it is hardly new or novel, but the implications of it are enormous. If history repeats itself, there must be clues about our future as we read the signs of times past. This suggests some amount of detective work.

During an investigation in a mystery story, or a real-life situation, one will often hear the recommendation to "follow the money." When investigating the future, it will be necessary to "follow the thought trends." You may agree with the observations in this book, or you may not. Whichever it may be, the counsel to follow the thought trends is still valid. We may even come to a similar conclusion in the end.

According to Heisenberg's principle of uncertainty in quantum physics, it isn't possible to know both the position (location) and the momentum (speed) of a particle at the same time. Sounds reasonable! Now, in our deliberations together, we will be exploring both the position and momentum of what appears to be a new era. Furthermore, we'll attempt to know both facts simultaneously. Does that seem like a mission impossible? Well, you'll probably admit, at least it does sound intriguing. So, let's begin.

We'll need to travel back to 1981, when an unusual and unexpected idea arrived. It happened this way. Ever since our marriage a few years earlier, my husband Glen and I often had new spiritual insights arrive on our mental doorstep. We would welcome and invite them in, but then carefully check out their "credentials"—ascertain if they were in line with our two textbooks on life.

Our main textbook was the Bible and the other a companion book that aids in unlocking the spiritual meaning of the Scriptures. The latter book includes a chapter titled, "Science, Theology, Medicine." These three were presented as modes of thinking and were also referred to as systems, with which we are all well acquainted.

8

Seemingly, "out of the blue," came the recognition that these three systems also represented eras in human history, and that each was taking a turn at being the predominant era. What an amazing thought that was! Could this be correct? As we reasoned it out and reviewed some historical facts, we could see the idea of rotating eras was plausible and even accurate. But, how could we back it all up? This was going to take careful thought and more enlightenment.

Up to that point, we had delved deeply into the spiritual realm, gaining more understanding of subjects such as prayer or spiritual identity. This time was markedly different, for the new inspiration was giving us an overview of the human scene—past, present and possibly even the future!

The next insight that arrived was that each of the three systems was a binary one, which meant it included two parts. The religious era was usually accompanied and supported by the government or the ruling power at the time. Great Britain with a monarch and the Church of England was a good example of that. But the medical era had the law as its underpinning, hence doctors and lawyers played a part together. The scientific era would be an economic one, in which scientists and economists walked almost hand in hand.

During that first influx of ideas, the actual dates of the eras were not obvious to us, but the rotation was. We could tell the religious era had already been supplanted by the medical and that the scientific sector was either already here or fast becoming the predominant system. Those observations and ideas would become more refined as usually happens with most of us. They were rather crude and embryonic at that point.

However, Glen and I felt secure enough in our new understanding to test it on a medical nurse, who came to look at our house, which was on the market. After a short conversation about her work, Glen said, "Your medical era will be overtaken by the scientific era," to which the nurse immediately replied, "It's already happening." And, so it was! That conversation took place in early 1982.

During that same decade, Glen remarked to me, "You think in titles." It appears he was prescient, that he had some foreknowledge of what my life would be like after his passing in 1993. Yes, it was only nine months after that sad occurrence that I became immersed in a totally new endeavor.

Suddenly, I found myself in the publishing business by bringing out a book my dad had written and left in manuscript form when he passed some years earlier. *The Ultimate Freedom* by John H. Wyndham is an inspiring wartime story, which met with immediate acceptance in 1994. It is still traveling slowly around the world by word of mouth being warmly welcomed by people of all religions or no religion. The interest was so great that translations in a few other languages were undertaken. This publishing activity opened the door for books of my own, including a couple of very unexpected musicals.

Glen and I had both given inspirational talks, many of them as a team. We also individually shared inspiration with others in our practice of spiritual healing. So, after his passing, I continued to share and develop the ideas. And I carefully watched the changing mental landscape, while taking on my new role as publisher and writer.

Some years passed during which books and music were written and published. One of those books, *Quiet Answers,* published in 2003, touched on the changing times and how the spiritual versus the religious movement was impacting churches. But it did not delve deeply into the era change. That idea sat on the back burner of my thinking, until it eventually moved to the front, mostly due to the decline in church memberships. Despite great effort on the part of churches, that downward trend continued. It was obvious that the mystery of the disappearing churches could only be solved by unraveling the mystery of a vanishing era.

In 2014, using the earlier insights and with further inspiration on the subject, I wrote a book on the eras that our world has been experiencing. It is titled, *Three Gifts: The Eras of Science, Medicine, Religion.*

As set forth in that book, some countries had already passed through an era and were on to the next, while others had not. This revelation, if we can call it that, explained why it is difficult to win certain wars. For instance, if a nation is fighting a religious war, their aim is quite different from a country which is in a non-religious or perhaps a scientific era. The peace-giving efforts another nation might bring to the fray are thwarted by that difference in era and aims. In the same way, the government, the health industry and religion have all been affected by the change in era, whether or not acknowledged.

The acceptance of an era change would impact every country and government, making a difference to their current decisions as well as plans for the future. But, this acceptance would come at a price, for change is so often resisted.

The change was especially difficult for the religious sector because, with the era of science upon us, the religious system had unwillingly retreated farther into the background. Oh, the religious element was still present, but it was no longer the predominant system or era.

However, there was not enough evidence in the '80s to convince the casual observer that this nation, the United States, and other parts of the world had indeed experienced a change of era, from the religious to the medical and then to the scientific. But, thinkers and writers had been noticing. The biographer Robert Peel wrote a book titled, *Spiritual Healing in a Scientific Age*, which was published in 1987.

Signs of the scientific era were all around us. From the 1980s on, the personal computer was gradually taking up residence in private homes requiring a room of its own known as the home office. There was obvious tacit agreement that we, in the United States, were in a scientific and not a religious period, and no one would have argued or suggested otherwise.

As technology increasingly took over almost every aspect of our lives, the inevitable conclusion was reached that we were indeed firmly settled into a scientific age. But the question of how and exactly when we arrived there has been slow to capture general interest or attention.

But, there have been some public acknowledgments. In 2015, just a year after my book on eras was published, Pope Francis made a startling statement in his address to the Catholic Church. He stated that "We do not live [in] an era of changes. We live [in] a change of era." This is a very important distinction in a very short statement.

Pope Francis had acknowledged not simply changing times, but an actual change of era! That was good news agreeing with my own findings, which were reported in *Three Gifts*. I believed that book on all three eras, and the direction they were taking, was complete. After all, no new era was in sight, or so it seemed. That is, until 2018 arrived. The signs of these times all point again towards a new era. And interestingly, they do not contradict the conclusions in *Three Gifts*. In fact, they corroborate and support them!

That is why, in 2018 and beyond, we have a mission which is twofold.

1. To find the location and type of the new era by understanding the preceding eras.

2. To pinpoint the times and dates of all the eras.

With those aims in mind, this book will first take a quick trip through the history of the three eras, the systems of religion, medicine and science.

The six little red buoys on this book's back cover will represent our six chapters. Though the ideas in this book were arrived at by diving deep into inspiration and research, you'll notice that the buoys are all on the surface. What a fitting symbol! The clues we need are on the surface and readily available to us all. Nothing is hidden. It is only the assembly—piecing the clues together—that will require a little effort.

Some may ask: Just how important is it to acknowledge a change of era, not simply changing times? Well, if that era change makes a tremendous difference to our way of living, our work, hopes, goals, our interactions with others and even world peace, then it is of great importance.

As we paint a miniature picture of the three eras, we will also pick up on the thinking of some key players. It's extremely helpful to not only highlight thought trends, but to put a human face on the eras as well. As we go along, I will also refer to other books I've written, that could help elucidate the subject at hand.

The question before us is: Where will we go from here? For a start, we can answer: We'll go from the religious era to the medical, and then to the scientific era. From there, we'll travel to the new era and beyond.

The First Red Buoy

Religion

The cover of this book, with its blue boat and red buoys, becomes a symbol for our travel. Perhaps the craft was a family fishing boat and the buoys were part of that activity. Whatever the purpose, the boat's simple appearance gives no hint of the magnitude of our search and of what we might eventually find.

The religious sector would surely be reminded of times long ago when a simple fishing boat became the focal point for Jesus' promise to his fishermen followers, "I will make you fishers of men."

For our expedition into the history of religion, we will begin by tackling that small first red buoy in the distance, which is quite appropriately placed, as the religious era is rather distant at this point.

One doesn't need to be a history buff to recognize that the religious era extended for such a long period of time. It was the predominant one and ruled the roost. In fact, it was the daddy, so to speak, of the other two systems—the medical and the scientific.

A quick overview here will suffice, but *Three Gifts: The Eras of Science, Medicine, Religion* deals in greater depth with the subject. That book is written as a novel with a storyline, which depicts a conference of the three systems to discuss why religion is declining and whether it will survive and continue with the other two into the future.

Attendees at the conference, set at a fictitious Thought Trend Institute in Santa Barbara, discuss this real-life problem while wondering why the three systems were invited. Surely, the decline in churches is a dilemma for the religious community alone to solve. Not so, as it turns out! They come to that conclusion through sometimes heated discussions, during which one participant from the science section even storms out the door. The participants did agree on the change of era, much to the dismay of the religious section. We can now vicariously join in their discussions by considering the history of religion.

The religious or theological era had existed from time immemorial up until the early 1900s. From earliest historical accounts, one learns of mankind's deep desire to attribute meaningful events to a divine power or being. It might have been the stars that evoked worship or even the animals found in cave drawings. Then again, statues made of wood or precious metals became objects of reverence.

Central biblical characters, such as Moses, ushered in a more spiritual worship, replacing the objects of worship with subjects. Loyalty, fidelity to what is good and the just treatment of one's neighbor became the Ten Commandments and laws by which to live.

Those guidelines deepened when the followers of Jesus Christ, being filled with his example and teachings, accepted that God is Love, and that our responsibility towards each other is to express compassion, brotherly love and forgiveness. Jesus had proclaimed, "I am come a light into the world, that whosoever believeth on me should not abide in darkness." For two thousand years, human society has been reminded of that light every year with Christmas festivities and promises of love, peace and goodwill.

Of course, the vast religious landscape, both Western and Eastern, was quite varied, and religion took many forms and many titles. Its history was somewhat akin to a wild roller-coaster ride, reaching high to sublime moments of revelation and the demonstration of spiritual power, then descending to the depths of the struggle for human power in what were termed "holy wars." And it was in this manner that the religious era prevailed for century upon century. Oh, there were many changes taking place within that era, but there was not a change of era itself until much later in human history.

Religion evolving

It appears that progress is a universal law that mankind must fulfill, because the three systems can be seen evolving regardless of which one is predominant at any given time. Religion's stages of development may be viewed in good part through the history of the Bible, so that is where we'll begin looking for thought trends.

There are two main elements of evolution found in the Bible, and they are the most important to consider in any religion. These are our first thought-trend clues.

What is the theology (the understanding of God or the Supreme Being) at any given moment, and therefore what religion (the practice of that theology) is taking place?

The answer to these two questions will reveal what kind of actions we may expect from others. People worship all kinds of things. It could even be their own body. In that case, thought would be devoted solely to the body and a strict regimen of diet and exercise might be religiously undertaken every day. Or, if someone's god is money, then they will diligently, constantly acquaint themselves with that god of gold and religiously practice the acquisition of it, regardless of how many toes they step on in the process. A nation with gold as their goal will likely go to war. To trace what mankind worships or their idea of God enables us to read the signs of the times. We'll consult the Bible again for thought trends regarding the people's idea of God and man's relationship to Him.

Firstly, the concept of God evolved from a rather wrathful, tribal Jehovah to the kindly Shepherd of David's twenty-third Psalm. Later, the New Testament portrayed the Supreme Being as our heavenly Father which is Spirit, and even as Love itself.

Secondly, man's relationship to God likewise evolved from his being almost the victim of a punishing deity, to part of a flock cared for by a tender Shepherd in the Book of Psalms. Likewise, Proverbs rejoices in the mercy of God and His help in dire situations. The old Testament ends with the telling question posed by the prophet, Malachi. "Have we not all one Father? Hath not one God created us?" This theme was carried into the New Testament and the teachings of Jesus Christ (also known as Jesus the Christ and Christ Jesus).

The three main monotheistic religions, teaching the existence of only one God, are Judaism, Christianity and Islam. They all originated in Arabia, in what is now termed the Middle East.

Because the influence of Christianity spread so quickly over the greater part of the globe, we will follow that thought trend in this book. The effect of Jesus' life and teachings was so enormous that the calendar was changed to reflect the date of his birth. Though some have questioned his great works and even his personal existence on this planet, yet one undeniable fact remains. The only reason we are speaking of the year 2018 is because of what Christ Jesus brought to the world.

Of course, there are other calendars which are recognized though not in worldwide use. In this year of 2018, the Aymara indigenous people of Bolivia celebrated the Andean new year of 5526. But most of the world runs on the Christian clock.

As might a comet from deep space, the impact of Jesus altered the direction of the world's rotation. Humanity was given the new axis of love on which to pivot. The logical conclusion would be that the advent of Christianity was surely the greatest thought change and revolutionary new trend in human history. Nothing quite like that ever happened before or has since.

According to most sources, the rapid spread of Christianity was due to three things. Firstly, was Jesus' theology of God's unconditional, impartial love; secondly was his compassionate care for the helpless and the needy (such as widows and children); and lastly the social networks of those days.

Let's look at these three points. Jesus' teachings will require some deep thinking if one is to gain their spiritual meaning, as they are so often in parable or metaphor form. However, the Sermon on the Mount is rather straightforward and obvious in its demands on us to live love without partiality. This is how the Gospel of Matthew records some of that message:

> I say unto you, Love your enemies, bless them that curse you, do good to them that hate you, and pray for them which despitefully use you, and persecute you;

> That ye may be the children of your Father which is in heaven: for he maketh his sun to rise on the evil and on the good, and sendeth rain on the just and on the unjust.

As for the second point of caring for those most in need (the poor, the disadvantaged or powerless), there is perhaps no better example given than in his parable in Matthew chapter 25. Jesus said, "Inasmuch as ye have done it unto one of the least of these my brethren, ye have done it unto me." More than kind sympathy, he taught active compassion.

Now, here is where the third point makes a dramatic entrance onto the world stage. It is the dissemination of

Jesus' message centuries after his ascension. And herein lies the problem for us today. In the telephone game, when a message is passed from person to person, the original idea can become garbled and misunderstood. This occurs with any idea passed down through the ages, including biblical teachings.

Instead of taking that wonderful light of love and shining it into every corner of a dark world, some have preached just the opposite and in the name of Jesus. That was certainly true of John Calvin, a dedicated man, whom many considered to be Martin Luther's successor. Evidently picking up on some metaphors Jesus used, and taking them literally, Calvin constructed his own version of the gospel according to Jesus Christ. He gave dire warnings in the mid-1500s, preaching salvation for the chosen few, who were predestined to go to heaven, and damnation for the rest, who were predestined to go to hell. His ideas spread across a good portion of the globe, instilling great fear in congregations.

Of course, his preaching on selective salvation flew in the face of Jesus' teaching that God's love is impartial for "he maketh his sun to rise on the evil and on the good." The willingness of people to accept such opposing beliefs at face value allowed Calvin's teachings to travel unchecked. They even reached the shores of the New Land.

Religion was central to the emerging nation, for America was founded on religious freedom. The church was the hub of a community and the subject of Divinity was taught at Harvard. Calvin's religious doctrines had found easy access into the homes of the settlers and into the homes and lives of their descendants.

In one of those homes lived a teenager named Mary, who would strongly oppose such an unloving doctrine. In fact, she would catch the spirit of the original idea of Christly love and run with it for the rest of her life.

Mary Baker was born in 1821 and brought up as a Christian in a devout Puritan home in New England. To this tender, loving and spiritually-minded girl, the teachings of Calvin were so cruel they made her literally ill. The family doctor, being called for, declared she was stricken with fever. Her mother urged her to go to God in prayer as was her habit, which she did. Mary later related the incident in her slim volume, *Retrospection and Introspection.*

> I prayed; and a soft glow of ineffable joy came over me. The fever was gone, and I rose and dressed myself, in a normal condition of health. Mother saw this, and was glad. The physician marvelled; and the "horrible decree" of predestination — as John Calvin rightly called his own tenet — forever lost its power over me.

The brave teenager had followed Jesus' counsel to pray "in secret," in the quiet place of one's own thinking. Such private prayer would be rewarded "openly." And it was!

Some years later, she searched for and found the healing power contained in the Scriptures. Her discovery explained why God is impartial and is Love as Jesus had taught. Her faithfulness was again rewarded and with a demonstrable understanding.

Mary Baker Eddy recorded her discovery in the book *Science and Health with Key to the Scriptures* first published in 1875. It is that book, which contains the chapter "Science, Theology, Medicine." Her discovery that there is a divine Science in the Bible, a Science whose Principle is Love, helped change the perception of so many, who thought of God as a punishing deity. The Science of the Christ, which Jesus practiced, was totally compassionate, and so Mary named it Christian Science.

This revelation of a divine Science unlocked the Scriptures and comforted a weary world. Countless people were healed just by reading the scientifically spiritual explanations in *Science and Health*, and churches sprang up in the wake of those healings.

Obviously, it has been mankind's concept of the Supreme Being that has been changing all throughout history and not Deity. Gone is the age-old concept of God as a man with a long white beard, just as the idea of a vengeful God is also disappearing. This evolution, or thought trend, is continuing. One may even notice changes in theology and religious practices by casual conversation with people we meet or with our close neighbors.

My mailman recounted that, though a dedicated churchgoer, he had never really read the Bible. But, due to a motorcycle accident and being laid up for a couple of months, he decided to take on that task. Through this study, he finally became convinced that there was no physical place called heaven or hell, but that they were states of mind. His findings are being echoed by others today. As we listen to them, we find "follow the thought trends" to be good advice and very revealing.

The mailman's conclusion, in conjunction with the ever-increasing acceptance of the idea that death is not fatal, is painting quite a different spiritual landscape than used to exist. Dogma, creed and ritual are waning. One's thinking and understanding are being given a place of much greater importance. A reasoned logical approach is taking over from the concept that belief only is sufficient to ensure one's own individual, spiritual future. But, what about the collective? What about the future of organized religion?

Organized religion receding

It would seem as though the trouble with church attendance is a current issue, but this trend began many years ago. During the early 2000s, churchgoers became painfully aware of what had been taking place for decades. It was difficult to overlook the attrition in memberships, and that churches of all denominations were either declining or closing. Small and mega non-denominational churches became the recipients of some departing members from mainstream churches, and their role expanded into meeting the social and civic needs of their congregations.

When did the decline of the churches begin? One Christian church openly admitted that attendance stood still in the 1930s and began dropping in the 1950s. Of course, as church attendance dwindled, questions and concerns grew. Who was responsible for this phenomenon? Truly, no one was at fault! No individual or church group was responsible for the change of era. But, it was much less demanding to simply encourage members to do better, promising they would attract new adherents, than it was to grapple with an era change. To admit that might even seem like giving up.

Church hierarchy has been faced with a dilemma, a Catch 22 situation. If they do not acknowledge the change of era, they could be blamed for not reading the signs of the times and for not preparing their flocks for a changed world. On the other hand, if they do acknowledge this, the flocks might leave at a more alarming rate. The pointed question would arise. Why struggle to keep our church buildings and services going if they are no longer the favored mode of transportation to heaven or even the means of persuasion for people to live good and decent lives? It is obvious why the subject of decline, along with the admission of a change in era, is avoided. For many, it has become the proverbial "elephant in the room." Church members know it's there, but they just don't talk about it.

However, not addressing the problem tends to hide the main reason for church organization in the first place. That reason has not disappeared. The idea of spreading the gospel or good news of hope, peace, love and healing is never out of style. It just may take a different form.

The love and compassion that we are supposed to be practicing towards each other can still blossom, as it never needed an organization to begin with. Diana Butler Bass wrote of experiential Christianity as the successor to the organized church in her book *Christianity after Religion: The End of Church and the Birth of a New Spiritual Awakening*. Christianity, freely lived in daily life, could continue.

Even as a flower turns to the sun, humanity naturally reaches out for a higher principle to life and for that better self we know to be present and available. The Golden Rule has not rusted away. Many businesses are advertising they operate according to that rule. A modern hotel chain promotes this very concept in an August 2017 advertisement: "At Marriott, we live by the golden rule and treat our guests the way we want to be treated with respect, care and compassion."

We could compare the religious situation with the decline of the horse and buggy. Transportation had not disappeared along with the buggy, but only that current form of it had. One was simply a means to an end. Being caught up in the means of forwarding an idea, instead of the idea itself, would eventually hide the idea and render one's efforts obsolete by not staying abreast of the times. The answer to mankind's yearning for something better and higher will arrive via different transportation today, if one is open to it.

We might agree the religious system could simply be in transition mode and that any attempt to evolve would be preferable to dissolving and disappearing. The question would be how to evolve. In the meantime, the religious sector is facing an uncertain future. Even during the few years since 2014, when *Three Gifts* was published, concerns have been multiplying. This is especially true in countries like the United Kingdom, where the nation's size makes the decline even more obvious.

In the hope of reducing some of that uncertainty and to provide a little comfort and hope, I undertook a car journey covering 1,500 miles through England, Wales and Scotland during the month of September 2017.

26

A telling tour

My dad's book *The Ultimate Freedom* showed how spiritual thinking can not only change lives but save lives too, even in a prisoner-of-war camp. And how he lived his life after the war is likewise inspiring, making his book an enthralling, spiritual adventure story.

This would be the encouraging message I'd take the churches and a few affiliated groups in the U.K. that had sponsored my talk tour. The reception worldwide to that book proves humanity is still seeking spiritual answers for their many needs. Surely this would bring them hope!

The talk tour was organized by Roma B., a dear lady in Surrey, England, whom I'd met only a couple of years earlier and who had attended some of my talks here in the States. Those talks were at a museum and a care facility in New England. Another was held in the home of a good friend, Marla C., who lives outside of Washington, D.C.

My new British friend expressed the desire to have me speak in her country. She felt the subject of my talk would bring hope to many there whose churches were on the verge of closing or had already closed. I promised I would come, if she would organize it. She went home and did just that, though it was unlike anything she had ever done before.

That is how I came to be standing in the living room of Roma's flat only six months later, hearing her son counsel her, "Now drive like a pensioner, not like Stirling Moss!" Yes, she was going to be doing the driving on this lengthy tour, and his caution gave me a heads-up about what to expect. Having lived for a couple of years in London during my teenage years in the 1950s, I recalled that Stirling Moss was a famous British race car driver.

Moss, who was knighted in 2000, had such a well-deserved reputation that it became common for the police, when stopping a speeder, to ask "Who do you think you are, Stirling Moss?" According to one account, that question really hit home when Stirling Moss himself was stopped and asked the same thing. Of course, he replied, "Yes." That took a few minutes to sort out, as you can imagine.

You may be wondering at this point why I am sharing these details, but there is a reason. It is to put a human face to the problem that the churches are experiencing. Church members, having put their all into working for God and humanity, were becoming increasingly bewildered and disappointed by the current situation. With the knowledge that the decline in church attendance was due to a change in era, how unkind it would be to allow those dear, dedicated members to feel like failures—that they had failed both God and man! The strong desire to help and comfort was the impulsion for the tour. Hopefully, the congregations would realize that the decline in memberships and churches had nothing to do with them. The era had simply changed!

The talk turned into a PowerPoint presentation and so Roma and I lugged all our equipment of cables, projector, computer and screen to each of our locations. (We were alone on our tour except for just one week when Marla joined us.)

Roma even found for me a wonderful drawing on the Internet of a green elephant sitting in a lounge chair, feet up, with a drink in one hand and a TV remote in the other. He was to represent "the elephant in the room."

The audiences were warmly welcoming and wonderfully attentive, as I recounted some of the inspiring results from the worldwide reading of *The Ultimate Freedom*. It had crossed all kinds of boundaries—geographical, language, religious and cultural. So many letters had been received, from all around the world, telling of lives changed and healed.

Truly, the world's hunger for spiritual solutions had not vanished or even declined! Towards the end of the presentation, we showed the elephant slide and I talked about the decline of churches and the change of era.

Each talk was on the same subject, except for the one given in Leeds, which was a PowerPoint presentation titled, "Reading the Signs of the Times," based on my book *Three Gifts*. Many came up to me after each talk saying they were so relieved, and that they no longer felt guilty or like a failure, because they could see the present religious situation wasn't their fault. The understanding of the times, or of any situation, is in itself a comfort. Roma and I were so grateful, feeling we had achieved a little of what we set out to do, to bring comfort and hope to a courageous, dedicated field.

Radio and television have provided a means for religion to spread its message for many decades. Now, the electronic church can be accessed from all parts of the globe at any time, day or night. Some of the churches we visited were already using those electronic means of communicating their message and for contacting their members. The main concern appeared to be about the brotherhood and how to maintain the joy of sharing with each other. The answer is not totally apparent, but small societies or networks of people holding common goals provide some clues.

Our trip was smooth in every way, as we traveled through the lush, green countryside of England and Wales up to Glasgow and across Scotland via Loch Lomond. We gave a talk in Edinburgh, then drove back down to the ancient city of York, where the last talk was given, before returning home to Surrey. The tour had included a total of eleven talks.

While passing through picturesque little towns, we'd catch sight now and then of a church edifice that had been re-purposed. One quaint tiny church was now a bridal shop and another a tea room. And there was a church that had become a dropping-in center for youth to receive help with current needs and spiritual guidance too. What an enlightening tour it was!

Later, I heard about a London church close to my heart. The wonderfully designed and massive church of my teens will be a performing arts center. The dedicated, smaller church membership moved into newly renovated quarters. The former structure is imposing, almost a fortress in appearance, while the new church premises have large inviting glass windows all across the front. The concept of religion is changing from something that stood majestically apart, to an offering that is now part of the mainstream of life! So, without the same building or membership, what was I actually part of for those two years of Sunday School in the 1950s? It was simply an idea that existed in time.

The obvious and undeniable changes in the U.K. brought home the fact that there has been a seismic shift in human consciousness, in both attitudes and interests. The pastoral landscape would remain as beautiful as ever, but the religious scene would never be the same again!

The Second Red Buoy

Medicine

Though we are now about to concentrate on the second to last little red buoy, which marks the medical era for us, we will not be leaving the U.K. quite yet. The TV series *Downton Abbey* was set in the countryside of England, and it contained clues to an era transition. In fact, it is difficult to fasten on a better example than that.

Downton Abbey was beautifully written, executed and acted. No wonder it became such a success in the U.S. as Americans do love all things English. There is a car parked near me with a license plate that reads "Born American, Brit at heart." I met the young girl who owns the car and she spoke of how she yearns to visit England. The *Downton Abbey* series transported us there to a different period.

The series portrayed the British upper class in their grand manor homes during the early 1900s. What lessons we learned from seeing the struggles some owners of the fine estates had in letting things go. One titled gentleman mourned over having to sell everything, including the wedding gifts he and his wife had received. "We held on too long, till there was nothing left." That said so much!

His era was changing from the religious to the medical, which was apparent in the many conversations held about the running of hospitals. The serving staff was leaving to take up work in offices and the trades. Inventions, such as the telephone and toaster, were being dubiously accepted while the horse-drawn carriage was joined by the estate's new automobile.

Now, returning to our cover, the medical system would undoubtedly view the blue boat and red buoys as symbolic of their efforts to maintain the human body and keep it afloat. But what is the history of medicine? Where did it come from before making its presence so strongly felt on *Downtown Abbey*? What thought trends had taken place?

Briefly, the rise of both the medical and scientific systems issued forth from religious beliefs and practices. I'll borrow from *Three Gifts* to make these points. The origin of medicine is described as one participant at the conference speaks:

> Apollo was designated the god of medicine, and so people turned to him for healing. And Apollo had a son, a god called Aesculapius. It is his rod with the serpent twined around it that is a symbol for medicine today. And if you follow the history of the healing arts there are gods and goddesses. The terms 'hygiene' and 'panacea' came from the names of two of the daughters of Aesculapius. Those goddesses supposedly represented health and a universal remedy.

Then there was an actual person, the Greek
physician Hippocrates, born about 460 years
before Jesus, and he was considered to be
the father of Western medicine. What really
shocked me was that the original Hippocratic
Oath began with, "I swear by Apollo the
Physician and by Asclepius and by Hygieia
and Panacea and by all the gods. . ."

As we can see, medicine had its roots in pagan worship
and idolatry. Religion and medicine in ancient times were
quite inseparable. Of course, the Hippocratic Oath has been
revised for modern times, and it no longer swears by the
gods or goddesses. That's a thought trend worth noting!

The unity of religion and medicine was gradually
dissolved as they both evolved, until they became considered
as separate systems in today's world. However, nurses in
British hospitals are still often referred to as "sister" harking
back to the nuns who ministered to the sick.

Now, let's explore a little of the history of medicine, but
first answer a question. How did Glen and I arrive at the
placement of the medical era? It was simply by a process of
elimination. We knew the religious era had passed, and that
the current scientific system had not immediately followed
it. So, something had to fill the gap in between. The only
remaining candidate in our trio was the medical system.

Mary Baker Eddy had explained the effect of medical
systems on the religious systems in her book *Science and
Health*.

The ancient Christians were healers. Why has this element of Christianity been lost? Because our systems of religion are governed more or less by our systems of medicine.

When medicine was increasingly taking over from religion as the predominant system in the early 1900s, that governing of the religion system became more obvious. Spiritual healing was even regarded with suspicion by the medical community. The medical era, being a binary system, which included lawyers, the law exerted its authority over the new-old form of healing. Was this form legal? Should it even be allowed?

Interesting isn't it that Jesus faced much the same questions in his time about his healing work though his was a religious period. His works ran counter to the current state of religion in the first century and, when these works appeared again, in the late 1800s, they again first ran counter to religion and then to the incoming system of medicine.

Medicine evolving

The crude medical practices of past centuries were gradually transformed into a more humane treatment of patients. The physicians themselves might well have been very tender human beings, but their practice was far from it. In fact, the modern progress of the medical system is seen at first in the care department, not in medical practices or inventions. The greatest shining light in caring for the sick or wounded was a woman in England.

Florence Nightingale (1820-1910) could have chosen a life of comparative ease and a place in British society, but instead obeyed a divine message she received in 1837. Of that she wrote, "God has spoke to me and called me to His service." She didn't know what the message meant at that time but, after caring for dying and sick townspeople during an influenza epidemic, she found her calling. It would be the profession of nursing.

When tending to the wounded soldiers in the Crimean War she worked tirelessly, even twenty-four hours a day. During her rounds at night, the only light available was a lamp she carried with her in the dark. Passing from cot to cot, she comforted and encouraged the wounded, earning her the title of "The Lady with the Lamp." It was said that grateful soldiers even kissed her shadow as it flitted by on her errands of mercy.

Of course, nursing was only part of the care given to patients, but Florence saw how important it was, especially in view of the current medical practice. *British Heritage* described that medical practice and her reaction to it.

> She began to notice that many of the popular treatments available—blood letting, administering infusions of arsenic, mercury, and opiates—were actually killing more patients than they saved. She believed and began proving she could save more patients from death by caring for their basic needs—keeping them warm, clean, rested, and well-fed.

Florence Nightingale's strong religious convictions became buoys to her work. She took her religion into the fields and hospitals. Her concept of God would surely have been compatible with a contemporary of hers in New England. Mary Baker Eddy brought comfort and light to the religious and medical scenes with the concept that all may pray to God, who is divine Principle, divine Love.

Florence Nightingale likewise comforted others with her strong sense of God's love. When a dying prostitute, whom she was tending, kindly voiced the hope that Florence would not experience the despair she felt, Florence replied:

> "Oh, my girl, are you not now more merciful than the God you think you are going to? Yet the real God is far more merciful than any human creature ever was or can ever imagine." (Wikipedia)

Under the heading of "Mercy without partiality" in *Science and Health,* Mary wrote: " 'God is Love.' More than this we cannot ask, higher we cannot look, farther we cannot go." Mary Baker Eddy's discovery of the Christ system of healing gave new impetus to the Scriptural declaration and promise that God is Love. She proved that Christian healing, which had been lost for centuries, was alive, well and still available. Her demonstrable discovery verified Jesus' teachings and showed the practicality of following his command to heal the sick. It also revealed the importance of thinking and its effect on the body. In her book *Retrospection and Introspection,* she wrote:

> During twenty years prior to my discovery I
> had been trying to trace all physical effects
> to a mental cause; and in the latter part of
> 1866 I gained the scientific certainty that
> all causation was Mind, and every effect a
> mental phenomenon.

The Mind she referred to is the divine Mind, God, also spoken of in the Bible. She saw that the human mind, which was the cause of sin, disease and death, had to give place to the divine Mind. The truth of being that lay in the divine Mind could be brought to bear on human problems just as invisible mathematics is applied to mathematical problems on the chalkboard. Healings of all types of diseases abounded through her teachings, and churches sprang up as a result of those healings, as already mentioned.

The continued union of religion and medicine carried on by Florence Nightingale was likewise maintained by her contemporary in New England.

Mary Baker Eddy (1821-1910) lived during the same span of time as did Florence Nightingale. Though geographically separated, they were united in their tireless efforts for mankind's health and happiness. Many interesting points of concurrence can be found in their lives. Mary also had heard a voice in her youth calling her. She too had a mission, yet to be revealed. She investigated different healing methods, being much in need of physical healing herself. One of these was homoeopathy, which distilled the medicine or pellet to such a point that no drug was left remaining. In that way, the pill became a placebo. Viewing the effects of this led Mary to conclude the improvement was due to the mental state of the patient and not the pill.

Florence was intent on giving her patients comfort and the right atmosphere for healing, thus acknowledging the part a patient's thinking plays in healing. Meanwhile, Mary was likewise concentrating on thinking as being integral to the healing process. No attempt will be made here to detail the life of this pioneer of Mind-healing, as Mary referred to the system of healing she discovered. Again, it was not the human mind, having caused the disease, that could cure the patient. It had to be a higher intelligence, the divine Mind, that would accomplish the healing.

Yes, Mary was making a huge contribution to the field of medicine. But this medicine was mental and spiritual, not material. It had no side effects other than to render the patient improved physically, mentally, morally and spiritually.

As Florence was writing papers on nursing, aiding in improving hospital conditions and teaching others the art of skilled nursing, Mary was writing a textbook on spiritual healing, teaching others to heal and setting up the first college for that purpose. She obtained a charter for The Massachusetts Metaphysical College in Boston in 1881. As stated in the Preface of her textbook, *Science and Health*, the charter was "for medical purposes." Again, this medicine was of a different variety, a spiritual one!

The field of nursing, in which Florence excelled, was by no means ignored by the discoverer of spiritual healing. Mary Baker Eddy saw the necessity for the tender care of the sick while they were undergoing treatment, whichever form of treatment it was.

The chapter "Christian Science Practice" in her textbook gives the overview of what is included in her mental (metaphysical), non-material form of treatment. A paragraph "Aids in sickness" includes comments on nursing. The habit of praying for God to take the patient to Himself could sound more like a farewell rather than a renewal. So, Mary began by cautioning against such prayers. She stressed the desire for healing by asking God to heal the sick.

> Prayers, in which God is not asked to heal but is besought to take the patient to Himself, do not benefit the sick. An ill-tempered, complaining, or deceitful person should not be a nurse. The nurse should be cheerful, orderly, punctual, patient, full of faith, — receptive to Truth and Love.

She made provision for Christian Science nurses in the *Manual of The Mother Church*, the Church she founded in Boston. You'll notice the similar tone to that general statement about nursing, though specific to her own system.

> Christian Science Nurse. Sect. 31. A member of The Mother Church who represents himself or herself as a Christian Science nurse shall be one who has a demonstrable knowledge of Christian Science practice, who thoroughly understands the practical wisdom necessary in a sick room, and who can take proper care of the sick.

Florence Nightingale is mentioned in *Science and Health,* and her amazing endurance is credited to the divine energy upon which she relied. Though involved in different systems of healing, these women were of a true sisterhood, and it's very possible that Mary felt this keenly. They were both bringing the light of love and compassion (exemplified by Jesus) to a world so in need of it. Mary gave her reason for naming the divine Science she discovered. "I named it *Christian,* because it is compassionate, helpful, and spiritual." (*Retrospection and Introspection*)

Those were the same qualities that Florence exhibited in her work, for her approach was compassionate, helpful and spiritual. Her writings are still referred to today, and she has been acknowledged as the pioneer of modern-day nursing.

Longfellow's poem "Santa Filomena" immortalized Florence Nightingale in verse, part of which reads:

> A Lady with a Lamp shall stand
> In the great history of the land,
> A noble type of good,
> Heroic womanhood.

In 1906, only four years before they both passed, Mary suggested that the magazine *The Christian Science Sentinel* should carry two drawings of a woman with a lamp on its covers. Longfellow's verse would appear with them. The cover was unchanged for over half a century when it was brought up to date, as Mary's counsel had been to "stay abreast of the times."

Though she had experienced wonderful results in the practice of Christian, spiritual healing, Mary Baker Eddy never suggested that the individual was without choice in the matter. One was free to choose a system and a physician. In her sermon titled, *Christian Healing,* Mary counseled:

> If you employ a medical practitioner, be sure
> he is a learned man and skilful; never trust
> yourself in the hands of a quack.

Mary also expressed her respect and expectation for the medical profession in these words found in *Science and Health.*

> Great respect is due the motives and
> philanthropy of the higher class of physicians.
> We know that if they understood the Science
> of Mind-healing, and were in possession of
> the enlarged power it confers to benefit the
> race physically and spiritually, they would
> rejoice with us.

If the physicians were not yet rejoicing about spiritual healing, they were certainly progressing in their own field of medicine. It was during a time of dire necessity that new inventions appeared on the medical horizon. Methods of testing and treatment, such as blood transfusions and x-ray equipment, took their place in battlefield hospitals during the First World War.

But it is in the history of hospitals themselves that we find the most compelling evidence for the changeover (and its date) to the medical era, as per this Wikipedia entry.

> All hospitals before the 1920s had operated without much money. Physicians donated their time, and costs for nurses and staff tended to be low. For the first time, hospitals required significant funds, just as doctors and surgeons began getting paid and nursing and staffing were professionalized. Many urban public hospitals recast themselves appropriately as major and, sometimes, highly regarded institutions, often establishing affiliation with universities and medical schools.

With proper funding and the professional aspect now in place, the medical system was coming into its own, and the religious system took a backseat. The new driver would be steering society for the next five decades. During that time, discoveries such as penicillin and insulin were made, and organ transplants became possible and even routine. Yes, medicine was now the predominant system.

While still in the twentieth century, though not yet welcomed in by the medical system, Christian healing was taken up by many Christian churches, and was no longer found only in the Christian Science Church that Mary Baker Eddy founded. That her discovery had exerted great influence was shown when Glen and I attended a holistic conference on healing early in the 1980s. Various denominations were given the floor. I well recall the Catholic priest, who freely admitted that his church was exploring Christian healing for two reasons. He said it was a biblical imperative, but it was also due to the challenge of Christian Science. And it was at that meeting, a clergyman introduced himself to us as a Christian Science Methodist.

During the same period, we attended a talk at a Lutheran Church. The pastor had an abundance of humor and humility as he detailed their many attempts to heal the sick. They were finally successful!

Though the field or system of medicine separated from that of religion, many individuals involved in those fields obviously did not relinquish one for the other. It is not unusual for doctors today to declare they pray for their patients, even while they treat them medically.

We can see the beginnings of a medical shift towards the importance of the patient's mental makeup in the holistic (mind-spirit-body) healing movement and in the following two instances.

The idea of the brain and mind being distinctly different is evidenced in the many NDEs (near-death experiences) we read about or watch on television. *Life after Life*, a book by Raymond Moody, brought the subject to public notice in 1975. Those who return from such a life-changing event usually possess a different view of reality. It is not unusual for an atheist after such an experience to become religious. The formerly-held concept that death is fatal is obviously being challenged by these accounts. Again, this thought trend is taking us higher and farther out of the limiting beliefs mankind had entertained about life throughout the ages.

If you read the Larry Dossey book *Reinventing Medicine,* published in 1999, you'll find he takes us through three stages and calls them eras of medicine. First was the obvious body orientation (where the patient was rather like a piece of meat to be inspected). Next is the mind-body connection (where the mental attitude or thoughts of the patient are taken into account). Finally, he advances to non-local consciousness, where the mind is not enclosed in the body.

Dossey is not alone in his observations, because many health care professionals are probing into the connection between the body and mind and are giving much greater credence today to the part that thinking plays. That field is most unlikely to return to the "piece of meat" concept, especially as they increasingly need to deal with the harmful effects of prescription drugs on mind and body.

A change of era and a time of invention

Now, the medical era was known for more than just its doctors and lawyers, which were usually the favored professions for little boys during that time. The changeover from the religious era to the one of medicine was marked by many new inventions. The automobile became the favored mode of transportation instead of the horse and buggy. Electricity finally was available even in agrarian regions of the country. The film industry blossomed along with the orange trees in California. Telephone lines linked states and countries. Cars rolled off the assembly lines in Detroit. Labor-saving devices put in a welcome appearance, and industry was changed forever by mass production.

Invention of one kind or another has taken place all throughout history, but there was a sudden influx unknown in former times. It was obvious that thinking had been liberated to attain greater freedom than ever before. Just 50 years after the discovery of the healing Science of Christianity in 1866, the religious era was in transition and found itself going out in a great burst of ingenuity and invention.

Decades later, the medical system would suffer the same fate of losing its status, as science took over the steering wheel in the 1960s.

So, questions could be asked: Did the medical system lose out in the transition to the scientific era? The only casualty that could be cited is the failure to pass satisfactory health care insurance, which was first considered during the medical era in the time of the Great Depression.

But, did the medical have the same problem as the religious sector? Did the medical system need comforting because it had been overtaken by science as the predominant era? Probably not, because the sciences basically took the medical sector under their wing. Biotechnology is a hybrid of medicine and technology. Today, much of medicine, or rather medical practice, falls under the heading of biotech, and the medical sector seems quite at ease with that union.

Rather than sorrow and concern about the future of medicine, there was more of a celebration taking place as the medical fell into line behind the scientific system.

So, what is the scientific era bringing to us? The question may better be asked: What is it *not* bringing?

The Third Red Buoy

Science

The scientific sector, on our journey to the future, would cast a quick glance at the blue boat and red buoys and point out how far the fishing industry has come. The use of electronic monitoring as to the whereabouts of fish, and the guidance systems to reach those fish, were now in place. Yes, they would undoubtedly view the scene through the lens of scientific invention.

Let's tackle the third buoy now and look at the sciences by borrowing again from the book *Three Gifts,* with its discussion on why the churches are declining. Please bear with these quick explanations of the origins of the sciences, as we will soon arrive at what one might term "the good part" which applies, of course, to us and our present lives.

A participant at our conference is speaking.

> And yes, there is a strong connection between science, religion and medicine, and it goes way back again to ancient times. Alchemy came from ancient Egypt where they practiced mummification and had a belief

in an afterlife and immortality. Alchemy was what was called a protoscience and it provided a platform for modern chemistry. It was actually a philosophy that eventually developed into the science of chemistry.

Naturally, to chemistry we will need to add the origin of physics. The quick explanation of that comes from another participant.

I've researched some history too and found that physics also had its roots in philosophy and in religion. It began as a study, or contemplation, of the natural world, that is, the material world and the elements that comprise it. Physics has a long history of evolving into what it is today.

As we skip further on in that book to the discussion of Sir Isaac Newton (1642-1727), you will probably notice that we are back in the U.K. again. Most know about this famous Englishman's discovery of laws of gravity, but don't recognize that he was a deeply religious man. He wrote unpublished reams on religion and wished to prove that God has a science. It would seem accurate to say that Newton's science came from his religion, just as medicine had come from religion.

Newton even pored over the Bible hoping to find hidden messages and scientific principles. At the conference, a budding young scientist shared his findings on Newton.

> Newton's main work *Principia* was titled, *Mathematical Principles of Natural Philosophy*. . . He believed God had designed the universe along the lines of rational and universal principles which were available for all people to discover. And that these principles would allow us to do well in this life not just hope for salvation in the next life.

Again, we have the sciences emanating from religion. If anyone had expected to find early strong distinctions between the systems of science, medicine and religion, they are doubtless disappointed by now. True, the three would evolve after periods of time and appear distinctly separate, but they certainly didn't begin that way.

The progress made by all three is also evident and in plain sight. From here on is where the plot thickens, or at least becomes quite interesting. Let's still remember the advice to "follow the thought trends."

Two falling apples

In the near or distant future, if a prize were to be given for the most scientific man of all time to whom would it go? Would it be Newton, Planck, Heisenberg or Einstein?

This was not a difficult question for Mary Baker Eddy, because she answered it in her book *Science and Health*. "Jesus of Nazareth was the most scientific man who ever trod the globe. He plunged beneath the material surface of things and found the spiritual cause."

This is where Newton came up short. Though he had diligently searched the Scriptures for clues of a divine science, he hadn't quite got there. Certainly, Newton had arrived at important conclusions about gravity, but had not probed deeply enough according to Mary Baker Eddy. She wrote in her *Miscellaneous Writings* under "One Cause and Effect:"

> A falling apple suggested to Newton more than the simple fact cognized by the senses, to which it seemed to fall by reason of its own ponderosity; but the primal cause, or Mind-force, invisible to material sense, lay concealed in the treasure-troves of Science. True, Newton named it gravitation, having learned so much; but Science, demanding more, pushes the question: Whence or what is the power back of gravitation, — the intelligence that manifests power?

However, Newton's universe still lay in the hands of God. "He has the whole world in His hands" was Newton's theme song for he had said: "The most beautiful system of the sun, planets, and comets could only proceed from the counsel and dominion of an intelligent and powerful Being."

During the plague, Newton had left Cambridge to stay at his mother's home in Lincolnshire. It was there, through a falling apple in her garden in 1666, that he received his first inklings of gravity. Two hundred years later, in 1866

Mary Baker Eddy was in New Hampshire catching her first glimpse of the science Newton sought after. The aftermath of a fall on the ice provided her breakthrough. She had called for her Bible and gained an insight into one of the healings Jesus had performed. This resulted in her own instantaneous healing, which she explained this way in her slim volume *Retrospection and Introspection*:

> My immediate recovery from the effects of an injury caused by an accident, an injury that neither medicine nor surgery could reach, was the falling apple that led me to the discovery how to be well myself, and how to make others so.

Mary Baker Eddy's discovery of a divine Science opened the door to a whole new world of Spirit with healing for humanity. She described a spiritual universe that was God-centered with man as the spiritual image and likeness of this divine Principle. Her discovery included synonyms for God, most of which are found in the Bible. They were Life, Truth, Love, Spirit, Mind and Soul, to which she added Principle.

The divine Mind or intelligence, named God, could be reflected by man but not appropriated as his own. The power still lay in the divine Mind, and this power healed. She had compassed all three systems in her discovery. Science, medicine and theology were all present and accounted for, as seen in the title of her work *Science and Health with Key to the Scriptures*. Some might object to uniting the three systems in such a fashion, but that is how they all began.

Progress in science

The advances in technology that the scientific era brought with it pose a problem. Where to begin describing this era? That's the question. Those advances since the scientific era settled in during the 1960s (we'll be more precise soon about the date) could only be called mind boggling to most of us.

Newtonian or classical physics had been joined by quantum mechanics (quantum physics), which enabled the creation of the atomic bomb, the computer, rocketry, lasers. telecommunication, space travel and exploration. Autonomous cars and incredible devices, that in former times would have been considered almost delusional ramblings, are on the horizon. Our computers and phones change so rapidly, it's hard to keep up. We might even wonder if our Smartphones are smarter than we are and need to consult a ten-year-old to be persuaded they are not!

Concerns have been voiced by both Bill Gates and Stephen Hawking concerning AI (Artificial Intelligence). Perhaps they envisioned a new takeover Hal, the computer that ominously starred in the blockbuster film *2001: A Space Odyssey*, which debuted in 1968. Here is what Hawking said in a BBC interview in 2014: "The primitive forms of artificial intelligence we already have, have proved very useful. But I think the development of full artificial intelligence could spell the end of the human race." Elon Musk, the CEO of Tesla stated in April 2018 that his company had relied too heavily on automation and robots for the manufacturing of their cars. He said, "Humans are underrated." We can all send up a cheer at that recognition!

Perhaps, we've each individually already had our own creeping doubts about the benefit of the many social platforms connecting us with each other. In proof, here's a humorous email making the rounds titled, "New Day."

Dearest Dad,

I am coming home to get married soon, so get your check book out. I'm in love with a boy who is far away from me.

As you know, I am in Australia ... and he lives in Scotland. We met on a dating website, became friends on Facebook, had long chats on Whatsapp. He proposed to me on Skype, and now we've had two months of a relationship through Viber.

My beloved and favorite Dad, I need your blessing, good wishes, and a really big wedding.

Lots of love and thanks.

Your favorite daughter,

Lilly

THE RESPONSE

My Dear Lilly,

Like Wow! Really? Cool!

Whatever ... I suggest you two get married on Twitter, have fun on Tango, buy your kids on Amazon, and pay for it all through PayPal. And when you get fed up with this new husband, sell him on eBay.

Love,

Your Dad

Oh, it's wonderful to connect with a friend on the other side of the world, and I for one wouldn't want to do without Skype. But could this trend go too far? What about the closer friends? It seems that we now have incredible international connectivity, but sometimes local loneliness. It's even been suggested that social media is making people anti-social. For that reason, France has banned mobile phones in their schools this year, so the pupils will interact with each other.

On top of that, we have virtual reality in the world of games, where players find themselves living a technological or virtual reality life!

But wait, for another question arises! What if this present human life is only symbolic, at its very best, of a perfect, spiritual life that is the actual reality? In that case, we'd have a virtual reality technological life about a virtual reality human life.

How fascinating, and how important to unscramble all of that! We can't be sure if we should really thank Planck, Heisenberg and even Einstein too for their contributions in discovering quantum physics. Newton appears somewhat blameless in this matter, but he had his own problems.

And who can forget the kind of humor that sprang into vogue after Einstein's theory of relativity took hold. An anonymous limerick gave us a taste of that.

> There once was a young lady named bright
> Whose speed was much faster than light.
> She set out one day
> In a relative way
> And returned on the previous night.

At this point, we'll take the proverbial tongue out of our cheek and get down to the serious business of exploring the scientific explorers.

In the 1980s, storage units and closet organizers appeared on the scene, because we ran out of space. As for time, we ran out of that too, when the busyness epidemic swept over society. "I'm just so, so busy" became the stock phrase. Yes, time and space were certainly being challenged. It is almost as though Albert Einstein's space-time continuum as the fourth dimension was being squeezed.

During that same period, games of chance became prominent by means of casinos and state lotteries. But on the flip side of hoping for good luck was fear that the unknown could strike, so insurance policies became the norm for everything we purchased. What had happened? Well, quantum physics had taken the center stage and spotlight away from Newton.

The predictable stability of a God-centered Newtonian universe was now challenged by an unstable, unpredictable seemingly man-centered, quantum mechanics universe. Our steady world now appeared to be run by chance.

Einstein wasn't too sure about quantum physics, though his own discoveries had contributed to it. He made the much-quoted statement about the uncertainty factor of quantum physics: "God does not play dice with the universe."

That our lives appear to be influenced by the physics of the day is enough to make us sit up and take notice, even if we have no desire to plunge deeply into the subject. So, let's not get too involved here, but just take a quick look over the scientific landscape.

Newtonian physics

There were three laws on which Newton founded his principles of natural philosophy. They were laws of motion, the law of inertia, and the law of action and reaction. These laid the foundation for what has been termed classical physics.

But his discoveries only took in big objects that were not very massive, and which did not reach the speed of light. In other words, they were on the macro or large, discernible level.

When it came to objects about the size of an atom in diameter, one had to enter the major sub-field of quantum mechanics. Now, we are on the micro level.

Quantum physics

While Newtonian physics was quite dependable, observable and even predictably unchangeable, quantum followed a different drummer. As already mentioned, Heisenberg's law of uncertainty stated that it was impossible to tell both the speed and the position of a particle at the same time. Almost in proof of that, we were given the puzzle of Schroedinger's cat that was alive and dead at the same time. The big game changer was the concept that the viewer could change the scene by the act of viewing it.

In a nutshell, Newtonian or classical physics deals with objects, the observable, but not with the mind of the observer. Quantum mechanics is inseparable from the mind of the observer and forsakes the objective sense of the universe for the subjective view. Perhaps this is the reason for the unpredictability of quantum, because the human mind is unpredictable and can change quite rapidly as it flits randomly from subject to subject. Random activity and chaos were the signatures attached to quantum physics.

Why does this matter to us? We're not in high school and won't be taking a test on the subject. Oh, but humanity is taking that test daily. We just don't know it.

It was in the 1980s that Glen and I became acquainted with quantum physics through a book recommended to us by a friend. *The Dancing Wu Li Masters* by Gary Zukov made the connection between quantum physics and Eastern religion. The Bantam Books edition came out in 1980 and listed the book under the New Age category.

Though one might not agree with his conclusions, the comparison Zukov makes between Newtonian and quantum physics is a clear, concise summary that is worth repeating here.

Dancing lessons for Newtonian physics

Can picture it.

Describes *things,* individual objects in space and their changes in time.

Predicts events.

Assumes an objective reality "out there."

We can observe something without changing it.

Claims to be based on "absolute truth," the way nature really is "behind the scenes."

Dancing Lessons for Quantum Mechanics

Cannot picture it.

Based on behavior of subatomic particles and systems not directly observable.

Describes statistical behavior of systems.

Predicts probabilities.

Does not assume an objective reality apart from our experience.

We cannot observe something without changing it.

Claims only to correlate experience correctly.

The act of viewing and changing what one observes has led some thinkers to conclude that we are creating our own reality, or that we are co-creators with God. However, a more scientific scenario would be to conclude that we are bringing into our experience what the mind dwells on, but this is not creating reality. If we are creating anything at all, it is simply our own experience and calling that reality.

For instance, in mathematics, we don't create mathematical reality. It already exists. We are simply either drawing into line with it or departing from it. In one case, mathematical harmony prevails and in the other case mathematical mayhem ensues. We have created neither the harmony nor the mayhem but have simply accepted one or the other. Now, back to quantum.

Quantum physics does not confine itself to the sciences but delves into the arts, medicine, religion and business. It appears quantum mechanics reaches into every pocket of human life and thought. The concept of the viewer being part of any process is echoed in the art field. The *Christian Science Monitor*'s article (Can an Algorithm be Art?) of May 8, 2018 on digital art, formed by a computer rather than by brush and paint on a canvas, contained this statement.

> One theory, put forth by French literary critic and theorist Roland Barthes in the 1967 essay "The Death of the Author," suggests that the viewer plays an integral role in realizing a work of art. Barthes urged the art world to expand the idea of "author" to include both artist and viewer.

To an author, questions must arise. What about copyrights? Will *War and Peace* be cataloged as authored by Tolstoy and his readers? Or to take it to the level of existential absurdity: Does a book or painting even exist if no one has seen it or read it?

Deepak Chopra suggests the combination of Eastern religion with medicine and a body based on a "quantum mechanical body." As for the workplace, can quantum physics be found there too? "Yes," according to a book published in 1992 titled *Leadership and the New Science* by Louise Wheatley. The bottom-up solution of the staff deciding on many issues shows the trend.

A bank manager, whom I knew twenty years ago, told me that she no longer could make the decisions because the staff was making them for her. I nodded and replied, "That's thanks to quantum physics."

When Newton gave way to Planck and quantum, the top-down leadership was suddenly out of vogue and even viewed as a dictatorship (which in some instances, it may well have been.) However, there is nothing to indicate that the collective can be more correct than an individual who might own the company and know it from the nuts and bolts to the finished product. It just seems that a democratic vote should prevail. But should it when the company is not employee owned? The workplace is still grappling with the question and wondering which works best, the top-down or the bottom-up approach in management.

This fascinating discussion is best left for another time, but the case has been made that quantum physics has entered into every facet of our daily lives.

Quantum physics, New Age and metaphysics

If Newton didn't go far enough to find the power underlying gravity, then the same thing could be said for Planck, Heisenberg, Bohr and others pioneering the field of quantum mechanics. In addition to that, another problem arose. Regardless of the scientists' intent, their discoveries, as far as they went into quantum physics, appeared to remove universal laws of science from under the control of God and hand them over to man and the human mind.

Conclusions, some classed as New Age, were drawn and propagated in films such as *What the bleep do we know?* The DVD *Copenhagen* depicted a possible, but fictional, conversation between Heisenberg and Bohr, who were pioneers of quantum physics and working on atomic power.

At the end, a huge mushroom cloud of an atomic bomb appeared and then the startling statement was made that quantum physics had given us a man-centered universe!

How did this reasoning come about? Let's consider the following. The idea of "like attracting like" can be found in quantum physics where particles known as quanta, or energy, are always in motion and vibrating at a certain frequency. These quanta tend to gather together with other like quanta, vibrating at the same frequency. Quantum physics is being touted as the scientific reason for why positive thinking and "like attracts like," seems to work. The basic concept is that our thoughts are constantly vibrating at a certain frequency and so attract other thoughts on that same frequency. The divine Mind is absent, and an individual's mind is responsible for all conditions, good or bad, which is not biblically or scientifically true. (Please see p.134 when you come to it!)

The human mind is the main feature in the positive thinking and in the New Age movements, and it certainly plays a conspicuous part in quantum physics. All of these have been placed under the term "metaphysical" and even "spiritual." This is where things can get a little tricky.

At this point, some distinctions need to be made. Metaphysics, the "science of the mind," as one dictionary has it, varies greatly. Metaphysics is a broad category for the mental realm and for the relationship of mind to matter. There are many types of metaphysics. There are Christian metaphysics and New Age metaphysics, which are entirely different from each other. There is likewise a difference between the metaphysics in Christian Science and in homoeopathy which is described in *Science and Health.*

> The difference between metaphysics in homoeopathy and metaphysics in Christian Science consists in this forcible fact: the former enlists faith in the pharmacy of the human mind, and the latter couples faith with spiritual understanding and is based on the law of divine Mind.

Because homoeopathy distills the drug down until there is nothing left of the drug (thus becoming a placebo), it does provide a bridge to the metaphysics of Christian Science. But, a bridge is not a destination!

If quantum physics removed all traces of matter from its theories, then it too may provide a bridge to the metaphysics of Christian Science.

The metaphysics in quantum physics relies on faith in the science of the human mind. But, the metaphysics in Christian Science "couples faith with spiritual understanding, and is based on the law of divine Mind."

I've heard it said by some that Mary Baker Eddy would have approved of quantum physics. It has been argued that its discovery was so new in her time, that she couldn't comment on it. Well, she may not have commented on it specifically, but she certainly did generically. The problem with quantum physics is that its metaphysics are entirely different from the metaphysics of Christian Science.

Which metaphysics will we choose? Which is accurate? There are a few elements involved. We'll look at our base of thinking first, and then reason from there further on the subject of quantum physics.

A change of base

To Mary Baker Eddy, the metaphysics of Christian Science, "based on the law of divine Mind," could never be coupled with matter, as that would produce a semi-metaphysical system and deprive one of a solid base from which to work. To this discoverer of a divine, spiritual Science, it would do no good to work in two bases at the same time. We'll take mathematics as an example. During the 1960s in college, I was required to learn "the new math" which included calculating in bases other than our usual base of 10. For instance, we learned that if we were using base 7 to describe the number 8, we would have to write 11. In other words, the 7 is a complete set or group designated by 10 and the extra 1 shows we have gone one number beyond that group. It's important to know which base one is working in. As it is in math, so it is in life!

Mary Baker Eddy saw that necessity as it relates to thought. In her textbook *Science and Health,* she explained that Christian Science changes one's base of thought.

> The effect of this Science is to stir the human mind to a change of base, on which it may yield to the harmony of the divine Mind.

This change of base for the human mind entails changing from a material base for life to a spiritual one. Quantum physics does not accomplish that change. Nor does reducing matter down to sheer energy (ethereal matter) necessarily constitute crossing over into the spiritually mental realm.

It's all too easy to inflate the metaphysics of quantum physics and thereby to conflate and confuse it with the metaphysics of Christian Science.

Viewed within its own system and the dictionary definition, quantum physics is a semi-metaphysical system, as it depends on matter and the human mind. Even if quantum physics eliminated matter and was accepted as a totally mental science, the human mind would still require a change of base, from the materially mental to the spiritual.

Within the metaphysics of Christian Science, quantum physics, which doesn't include the divine Mind in its calculations, would not even rate as a semi-metaphysical system. That fact is deduced from the following in *Science and Health:*

> . . .semi-metaphysical systems afford no substantial aid to scientific metaphysics, for their arguments are based on the false testimony of the material senses as well as on the facts of Mind. These semi-metaphysical systems are one and all pantheistic, and savor of Pandemonium, a house divided against itself.

Semi-metaphysical systems and pantheism

Semi-metaphysical systems are pantheistic! This is such an important fact to realize and remember. The link made by Gary Zukov between quantum physics and Eastern religion is accurate enough depending on how we view quantum.

Eastern religions tend towards the idea of God in everything and everyone, which is pantheism. Quantum physics appears to travel in that same direction, with the viewer changing the view. Picking up on that, you'll hear, "It's all subjective" or "It's all in you" or "You are creating reality." Following that thought trend has led some to proclaim they are co-creators with God or even further state, "I am God." What problems come from such reasoning!

This is where the biblical concept of man, in the first chapter of Genesis, made in God's "image and likeness" comes to the rescue. Christian Science fully supports that with the explanation of a mirror's reflection. The image does not contain any power within itself but simply reflects what the original does. Jesus said it when he firmly stated, "I can of mine own self do nothing." Pantheism teaches that man contains the power, not reflects it. Christianity gives all power to the divine cause. Christian Science states, "All substance, intelligence, wisdom, being, immortality, cause, and effect belong to God." (*Science and Health*)

It all seems to boil down to cause and effect. Newton had a cause and effect universe, with God as the cause. If man were absorbed into God, so losing his identity, we would have an all-cause universe.

Human reasoning deduces from quantum physics that cause is within the effect (God is within man), or in other words, a pantheistic, all-effect universe.

Christian Science logically teaches that the greater cannot be in the lesser, so to believe that God could be in man would be impossible, as God is greater than man. The cause is greater than the effect. There can be only one great and true cause, God, of which the spiritual universe, including man, is the effect. "Christian Science explains all cause and effect as mental, not physical." (*Science and Health*)

To pursue this subject further, it's helpful to read, in its entirety, Mary Baker Eddy's Message to her Church in 1898, titled *Christian Science versus Pantheism.*

There is also an excellent, explanatory pamphlet "Christian Science and Eastern Religions" by Howard Palfrey Jones, which is available on Amazon. Jones was a journalist turned diplomat and the American ambassador for Indonesia during the Eisenhower administration.

Jones wrote about the amazing feat of walking on hot coals by youth at a wedding in San Francisco in the 1960s due to the influence of Eastern religion during that period. Jones also cites the Eastern religions and their basic differences from Christian Science.

A Crowning Solution

Now, it has been said that quantum physics gave us a man-centered universe. However, that assumption is not in consonance with Planck's own view, because he stated, as per a Wikipedia entry:

> Religion and science demand for their foundation faith in God. For the former (religion), God stands foremost; for the latter (science), at the end of all thought. For religion He represents a basis; for science, a crowning solution towards a world view.

That scientific "crowning solution," (being God) could not possibly reside in a man-centered universe. Therefore, quantum physics appears to be the human mind's attempt to explain God's universe.

We'll return to this subject, as we attempt to crack the quantum code in our final wrap-up. But, for now, here's a logical question. What can we learn or gain from quantum physics?

We could agree that the field of quantum physics has opened a door that had been closed in classical or Newtonian physics. It is allowing for the human mind to take a scientific part in the universe, just as the doctor is allowing for the patient's mind to be of some consequence in the field of medicine and healing. Like the mind-spirit-body holistic approach found in medicine, perhaps quantum physics is a somewhat holistic approach to the sciences.

To gain a more mental or metaphysical view of the universe, including man, is a step forward, and it could be the precursor to understanding a totally spiritual, mental universe under the law of God.

We may wonder: How far will the sciences go? They will certainly continue to explore all kinds of alternative energy, as energy is at the basis of quantum physics. But there is a larger question. Will they forsake the one foot on the side of physics and plant both feet on the thinking or metaphysical side?

Perhaps, as we follow the clues in the telltale dates and then peer into the future, we'll find an answer or a thought trend worthy of investigation.

.

The Fourth Red Buoy

Telltale Dates

Let's just recap for a moment to see where our exploration has taken us. We've acknowledged the part that thinking, not only faith, plays in religion. That we should "know the truth," as Jesus promised, is undeniably a thought process and might be termed faith elevated to spiritual understanding. The medical system has moved over to some degree to accommodate thought as part of its practice. The sciences with their telescopes and measurements find themselves unlikely bedfellows with the observer who, through thought alone, is changing the subject or object of their interest. Thinking is on the march!

At last, we arrive at the transitions. The mystery of the eras, if we could call it that, is solved by the telltale dates. At least, that was my falling apple.

To have 2018 suddenly appear with so many of the same issues and earmarks as 1968 was very surprising to those who well remember the former time. Yes, only a few months into the year, the co-incidences were screaming for attention, and they certainly captured mine. The three main issues of 1968—the youth, women and civil rights—were suddenly being played out again and very early in 2018. What could this all mean?

Questions were plentiful, but answers were appearing too. It was all adding up like a giant jigsaw puzzle, with important pieces that suddenly fit perfectly. For instance, on close inspection, we find that a higher humanity was evolving through improved thought trends. We might think of this life journey as one driving up a mountain. The road does not simply go straight up but out of necessity winds around, and the traveler will come to what appears to be the same place, though it is higher up the mountain each time.

How long did it take our world to make the circle around the mountain? Fifty years is the candidate, because that is how long it took for the same signs to appear again, from 1968 to 2018. And there had to be a crossover or transition time, not a sudden cutoff. According to popular wisdom, it requires thirty years for something new to catch on. such as the automobile taking over from the horse and buggy.

While strong evidence has been found for such a lengthy crossover time concerning the eras, it is simpler to focus on a ten-year period, such as the decade of the 1960s, which has been pegged as 1963-1973. The years before our target year of 1968 were leading up to the change, and the years after were cementing that new direction.

If 1968 was a pivotal year for a change of era, perhaps that could be said for 2018 as well. If so, what new era would emerge? And what about the past? Counting backwards, if 2018 is to be another pivotal year and only fifty years after 1968, did that point to 1918 as the peak or changeover year for the previous era?

I'd been hoping to pinpoint a time, period or date for the emergence of the medical era. We can now zero in on the ten-year period of 1913-1923, peaking in 1918 at the end of the First World War, as the changeover from the religious to the medical era.

At this point, we'll start inspecting the three transitions of the eras, but only briefly. Perhaps there should be a warning label for the reader as many events will be extremely disturbing.

The years around 1918

Youth

Although there had been a successful newspaper boys' strike in New York City in 1899, in general the youth of that era had no voice. If indeed they had one, it could not have been raised in protest of the ongoing war, for the Sedition Act of 1918 (repealed in 1920) made it illegal to criticize the government during war years. There was, at that time, an ongoing concern about children's health and well-being, for they worked long hours and often in deplorable conditions.

An act in 1918 directly and negatively impacted children in the workplace. Hammer v. Dagenhart was a U.S. Supreme Court case in which the Court ruled in favor of Dagenhart, nullifying the Keating-Owens act, which attempted to regulate child labor. Without that protection, the Court virtually consigned large numbers of children to the textile mills. The treatment of these children, amounting to child abuse and even slavery, continued unchecked for twenty more years.

The adult community would eventually raise its voice and conscience to protect children through later legislation, but the youth themselves were generally muted. "Children should be seen and not heard" was the accepted norm for society, and it would take a revolution to change that situation.

Women

Seneca Falls, N.Y. was the site of the first meeting for women's rights in 1848. Women have endured much over the many years of struggling for the vote. Here is what happened at the Occoquan Workhouse on what has been dubbed "The Night of Terror," in 1917. Thirty-three suffragists from the National Woman's Party were arrested while picketing outside the White House for the right to vote. Forty-four club-wielding guards beat, kicked, dragged and choked their charges. Women (one was 73 years old) were lifted into the air and flung to the ground.

In 1918, due to increasing public pressure, President Wilson publicly declared his support for a federal women's suffrage amendment. The House of Representatives passed it by a two-thirds majority on January 10. But the Senate was slow to act on it, so women continued their protests by holding open-air meetings in Lafayette Park in Washington, D.C. on three occasions in August of 1918. Each time they were arrested, tried, convicted and sentenced to time in the old District Workhouse. Two more years would pass before women first voted across the U.S. on November 2, 1920.

Alice Paul wrote and introduced an Equal Rights Amendment (ERA) in 1923, aimed at providing women with the same opportunities as men. This has yet to be completely ratified by enough states to place it into law.

The mighty struggles and terrible abuse of women could be termed the forgotten history of the Suffragette's Movement. It is now simply known as the First Wave of Feminism. Surely, the greatest discrimination in most cultures around the world has never been racial. It has been gender! Women are still fighting to come out of the shadows and their role as second-class citizens.

Civil rights

After the Emancipation Proclamation of 1863 by President Lincoln, there was still much needed to free the slaves in the U.S. Amendments were made to the Constitution in the following years to forward the cause of human freedom, but the human heart could not be so easily amended, and injustices prevailed. There was not much activity to promote equality on the civil rights scene during the years surrounding 1918. In fact, just the opposite.

The terrible practice of lynching black men, and even black families, was not uncommon and was most prevalent from 1890 to the 1920s. This punishment could have been for some slight social infraction such as possessing a photo of a white woman or walking behind a white man's wife.

A memorial of the moral darkness of that time would appear a century later in 2018. The details of that earlier period are too sad and cruel to relate, and the only thing that can solace us is the fact that we have moved past that period in history and are on an upward trend. Oh yes, there is much farther still to go, and that cannot be denied, but we can see some improvement and for that we can be grateful.

To put it into some perspective, let's now look at the golden thread running throughout history.

The Golden Thread

No matter how dire the circumstance may be on the human scene, there always appears to be a golden thread of goodness—the desire for a higher humanity—running through the narratives. (Humanity can mean humankind or the higher, better instincts and feelings of mankind.)

For instance, slavery of many kinds and of various races was an issue being confronted long before Jesus appeared. In the sixth century B.C. the Athenian lawgiver Solon abolished slavery for debt and freed all Athenian citizens who had formerly been enslaved. In more modern times, slavery was abolished in France in 1794, in England in 1833, and in Hawaii in 1852.

Efforts for reform can be traced over ages and continents and have been met with varying degrees of success. Though progress was often just incremental, it was progress nevertheless. Each of the categories we have just considered is returning again and again, obviously until we get it right!

It was fifty years after the Emancipation Proclamation that the years surrounding 1918, the crossover time from the religious to the medical era, revealed the deplorable state of youth, women and the black race. It was as though the problem needing a solution was laid bare before the nation and a gauntlet thrown down with the challenge: "You wanted a nation of equality and freedom for all. You've fought for it and established it on that basis. Now, prove it!"

Alexis de Tocqueville, the French diplomat, historian, political scientist, and author of *Democracy in America* stated: "America is great because she is good. If America ceases to be good, America will cease to be great."

The golden thread of goodness can be seen winding its way through human history, because there have been those willing to purchase and pay the price for it, though it be with their own lives.

An era-changing year

The year 1968 has always been a stand-alone year according to history books and commentaries. It's considered one of the most tumultuous years in U.S. history. One newspaper stated, "It cast a long shadow." Many years ago, Tom Brokaw in a TV program asserted that 1968 was the year that separated the past from the future. That certainly was a good clue pointing to the change of era.

In May 2018, a TV documentary on 1968 was advertised as, "A year of seismic shifts in American politics, social movements, global relations and cultural icons that changed the modern landscape." Another TV program simply announced it as "The Year that changed America." Even in so many families, including my own, it was a year of much change. For all of these reasons, 1968 appears to be the perfect candidate for the office of era changer.

By investigating the time spans, one will find the acceleration happening in the five years prior to the pivotal date and the ensuing five years as cementing that direction, as already mentioned. *American Heritage* pinpoints the 1960s as taking place from 1963, beginning with the John F. Kennedy assassination, and ending with 1973's Yom Kippur war and the oil embargoes. Events simply reached a climax in 1968 in the middle of that decade.

So many influences appeared to be at work during that period and following the thought trends was not simple nor linear. It took me thirty years to figure out, to my own satisfaction, just what did happen in the '60s.

Marked by two high-profile assassinations, that of Robert Kennedy and Martin Luther King, Jr. and a multitude of protests, 1968 reached a peak of notoriety. However, that peak is shrouded in clouds and mystery, if it is not recognized as the sign of an era taking hold. The year 1968 was the tipping or pivotal point for the scientific era and there was no going back. It is as though the announcement was made, "From now on you will refer to this age, this period, this epoch, this era, as a scientific one!"

The years around 1968

Youth

Three distinct thought trends can be seen during this time. One was the youth's resistance to the Vietnam war. "Hell no, we won't go" was the chant often accompanied by avoiding the draft as some of the youth fled to Canada. Protests took place mainly on college and university campuses, such as Columbia, Stanford, Kent State and Berkeley, though the Berkeley protests were mixed with an issue over land known as the People's Park. Reasonably peaceful "sit-ins" were held on occasion, but students also clashed violently with the police resulting in fatalities.

The second thought trend was the rejection of authority of all kinds, including governmental and parental. The anti-establishment, anti-war youth did go to war—against their parents. The extreme resistance to parents in the 1960s was dealt with in my book *Quiet Answers* under the heading, "The saddest of all wars." To quote that book, "The fallout from the war on parents lies like atomic waste scattered over the juvenile landscape of today."

Not surprisingly, the child/parent relationship changed dramatically as evidenced by the sad statement of one man, who complained he was a member of the silent generation. He grew up being told to listen to his parents and later, when he became a parent, he was counseled to keep quiet and listen to his children. So, according to him, he never had the chance to speak. Yes, parenting suffered greatly during that period of youthful rebellion and has never been quite the same since. We'll revisit this subject a little later.

Thirdly was the youthful desire to upend the status quo as seen in the hippie movement, which was full of wild abandon. Youth flouted the social norms as they became "flower children," who freely partook of drugs and sex. The institution of marriage was undermined by the onslaught of "free love," as youth made the peace sign while chanting, "Make love, not war." The 1969 festival at Woodstock,

N.Y., a graphic depiction of the new attitudes, has been immortalized in music and film as being a pivotal part of the counterculture of that period.

Women

The Feminine Mystique, a book written by Betty Friedan and published in 1963 was instrumental in giving voice to the Second Wave of Feminism in the U.S. That wave then spread across to Europe and other countries. During the 1960s, women's rights were being strongly debated under the heading Women's Liberation Movement.

Of that period, Donna Brazile, the CNN contributor and Democratic strategist wrote: "It was in 1968 that 'women's lib' became an official part of the societal shift, the tide of change toward economic, social and legal equality. (The name "women's liberation" came from a nationally circulated newsletter that came out of Chicago.) It was a time of consciousness-raising, and women refused to be left out."

Hardly a time of quiet interchange of ideas, strong rhetoric permeated society. The term "male chauvinist" and even "male chauvinist pig" as a reference to men was in free use during the '60s and '70s. Again, extremes were obvious as evidenced by "bra-burning" episodes.

The ERA was still being debated and it passed both houses of Congress in 1972 but needed ratification by 38 states. This has yet to happen. It was obvious that the march for women's equality, with strong language or quiet efforts, would continue. During the 1970s, Ruth Bader Ginsburg took on and won many cases of discrimination against women. She would become a Justice of the Supreme Court in 1993, only the second woman to hold that position.

Where the earlier period around 1918 contained the struggle for the vote, this new period was demanding equality of job opportunities and equal pay for women. One stage built upon the last. The road around the mountain had come to the same spot once more, but now a little higher up.

Civil rights

The modern seeds of resistance to injustice were sown by many including Rosa Parks, a black woman who refused to give up her seat to a white man in a crowded bus in 1955 in Montgomery, Alabama. For that and her other activist efforts, Parks has been called "the mother of the civil rights movement."

Martin Luther King, Jr., according to Wikipedia, was "an American Baptist minister and activist who became the most visible spokesperson and leader in the civil rights movement from 1954 until his death in 1968. King is best known for advancing civil rights through nonviolence and civil disobedience, tactics his Christian beliefs and the nonviolent activism of Mahatma Gandhi helped inspire."

Just as women had been formerly jailed for their suffrage campaign, so King was also jailed for his efforts.

In 1963, the March on Washington, D.C. for Jobs and Freedom took place, at which King gave his famous "I have a dream" speech. He followed that with a rousing plea to "let freedom ring," concluding with these stirring words:

And when this happens, when we allow freedom to ring, when we let it ring from every village and every hamlet, from every state and every city, we will be able to speed up that day when all of God's children, black men and white men, Jews and Gentiles, Protestants and Catholics, will be able to join hands and sing in the words of the old Negro spiritual, "Free at last, free at last. Thank God Almighty, we are free at last."

Civil rights came into sharp focus after King's assassination at a motel in Memphis on April 4, 1968. Four days of riots followed the assassination. The peaceful proponent of non-violence, which Martin Luther King Jr. surely was, had met a violent end. However, his legacy lives on, and his statement that death could not stop the struggle for equal rights has proven true.

A six-day march on Washington, D.C. was not only a reaction to that tragic event but was intended to highlight the plight of the poor and those discriminated against. The same year, many issues of race were brought to the surface. For instance, the long struggle involving equality in housing culminated in the Fair Housing Act, also known as the Civil Rights Act of 1968.

2018

In the first few months of 2018, marches of some significance had already taken place in Washington D.C.

concerning the youth, women and civil rights. It is as though the year just couldn't wait to get started on its upwards mission to achieve a higher humanity and to open a new chapter or era for the country and the world.

Youth

On March 24, youth streamed into the city and assembled in a "March for Our Lives." They protested the lack of safety in their schools, which in the past were considered to possess almost sanctuary status. That status has been violated many times by shootings at schools across the country.

The gun violence in Parkland, Florida galvanized the survivors of that school attack, which left 17 dead, to take their plea for greater gun control to Washington, D.C. The outcry, for school safety and new gun measures, continues in various forms and forums. It will not disappear quickly nor quietly! The concern for school safety has been joined by another equally dire need concerning children.

In June, a crisis of conscience swept across the U.S. due to the "zero tolerance" approach to the immigration problem. This meant that children were separated from parents crossing illegally into the U.S. The recorded cries of these children provoked such an outcry from citizens, and religious communities, that the president signed an order on June 21st to stay this practice and keep families together, at least for the moment. That is still to be fully implemented.

The youth of today desire equality, especially in pay, bringing increased interest in employee-owned businesses. A living wage fell victim to corporate profits. some time ago.

For an employee to work full-time and yet not to receive a living wage doesn't seem right. When that situation is rectified, the standard of living and happiness will rise immeasurably. This is not a political but a moral issue. Our democracy should support the worth of everyone.

As a result of these current times, fearful concerns among the American youth are being answered in part by college and universities with courses on happiness. Dr. Laurie Santos of Yale teaches the most popular class on campus. It is under the Science of well-being, centering on happiness.

Women

There were two rousing marches for women's rights beginning on January 19th and 20th of 2018. Women wearing pink hats formed a sea of protesters on the second annual March for Women. The first march was in January of 2017, when a total of 4 million worldwide had taken part in a protest when Donald Trump was inaugurated as President of the United States. The second protest in 2018 had picked up steam and included immigration, healthcare and racial divides.

In addition, women's voices were no longer silent about the practice of sexual harassment and abuse in the work place, or any other place for that matter. Abuse within families was likewise exposed.

The #MeToo Movement grew, and is still growing across the globe, as well-known and trusted names are added to the list of those who have experienced the abuse. Sexual crimes are not contained within national borders.

Despicable acts by those possessing prominent positions in areas such as business, medicine, sports, religion and entertainment are no longer cloaked in secrecy or protected by status. Society's guilty little secret is out! Humpty Dumpty has fallen off the wall and can't be put back together again, not even by all the king's horses and all the king's men! "The king's men," those in a position of power, can no longer protect the abuser or be the abuser.

Gihon, a river in Genesis, is defined in *Science and Health* as, "The rights of woman acknowledged morally, civilly, and socially." This river of thought keeps on rising!

Civil rights

In Washington, D.C., a candlelight vigil was held on March 4, 2018 to commemorate the assassination of Martin Luther King, Jr. in 1968. It came under the banner of the "People's march for justice, equality and peace," and many religious denominations were represented.

On April 26, 2018 the National Memorial for Peace and Justice was launched in Montgomery, Alabama. The memorial is known informally as the Lynching memorial, which records that terrible crime against humanity.

"The Black Lives Matter Movement" began in 2013 (within our exploratory time zone of 2013-2023) due to the police shooting of a young black man. The growing movement protests racial profiling and discrimination.

In February and March, as part of its social justice focus, The First Unitarian Church in Virginia presented its *Second Annual Black Lives Matter Art Exhibition.*

Youth, women, and civil rights

A vigil and march, which addressed all three areas of concern, was held before the year was even at its midpoint.

On May 24, 2018 a service and candlelight vigil were held at the National City Christian Church in D.C. with a procession to the White House. All told, 2,500 people participated in person in the service and procession. A six-point document was read both at the service and again outside the White House.

The document's title was "Reclaiming Jesus" which acknowledged Jesus' teachings on care for the needy, for women and children and those marginalized by society. It claimed that our current governmental decisions and practices in 2018 run counter to those teachings. The six-point document was drawn up by Reverend Jim Wallis, President and Founder of Sojourners, and signed by twenty-two religious organizations.

Drastic changes are taking place within the religious community itself. On June 12, 2018 the Southern Baptist Convention held its annual meeting. On June 16, the monthly magazine the *Atlantic* reported on the meeting and that the SBC is breaking with past practices and with the Republican party. A contributing factor to the change of direction was a statement signed by 3,000 women disputing the concept that they must submit to abusive husbands. That cruel interpretation of the Bible was no longer valid.

In consonance with their changed direction, the SBC elected a new young president, Rev. J. D. Greear. And quite surprisingly, the new and the old path were both revealed.

The *Atlantic* reported that Greear promised to lead the denomination down a different path, which, he said, must include efforts both to repent of "a failure to listen to and honor women and racial minorities" and "to include them in proportionate measures in top leadership roles.'"

Jonathan Merrit, the reporter, then gave the history of the conservative mode that was being replaced. His explanation of what promoted that ultra-conservative viewpoint reads almost like the plot of a movie. He wrote:

> In 1967, at New Orleans' historic Café du Monde, a young seminary student named Paige Patterson and Texas Judge Paul Pressler met over a plate of beignets to hatch a plan to unite conservative Southern Baptists and take over America's largest Protestant denomination.
>
> The two men successfully executed their strategy in the subsequent decades, a movement they labeled the "Conservative Resurgence" and their opponents dubbed the "Fundamentalist Takeover." Whatever one calls it, the result was a purging of moderates from among denominational ranks, the codifying of literal interpretations of the Bible, and the transformation of the Southern Baptist Convention into a powerful ally of the Republican Party.

It's clear that the seeds of that ultra-conservative movement were sown during the last change of eras in 1967, a time of extremities. An overturning of that extremity is taking place as we enter this next era in 2018.

Honest history telling can explain so much. In fact, the *Atlantic* article cracked open a "cold case" for me. During the 1980s, concerned parents talked with Glen and me about the wave of religious fundamentalism that was separating families. Grown children would sometimes sever ties with parents and other family members, because their families were not "saved." The grieving parents had no idea what was going on, and neither did we at the time. A young member of our own family went through that period and wouldn't even speak to us for two years.

I'd always wondered what happened, because the situation seemed to arrive out of nowhere. But things do have a way of coming to the surface, don't they!

We can't deny the moral courage the Southern Baptists have displayed in changing their extreme religious direction and in abandoning their political agenda. However, one might surmise that the huge decline in church membership— losing one million adherents since 2003—also provided impetus for a change.

As the decline continues for mainline religions, there will be of necessity further soul searching and deep contemplation as to the future of religion in general.

Watching the thought trends, reading the mental signs of our times, will be of even greater importance in times to come. For that reason, the following discussion on thought control will be included.

A Telltale Sign

Control thought or thought control

At this point, our telltale signs have all had dates affixed to them showing the issues and the progress over the years. There is another telltale sign that has no date, and which can take various forms, both overt and hidden. It's the subject of mind control. Perhaps the film *The Manchurian Candidate* comes to mind, or the ominous prospect that technology will one day attempt to control our thinking.

It's easy to dismiss these notions as hardly relevant to us, but we are bombarded daily with advertising which attempts to control what we purchase, or which suggests how we should live our lives. Worse still is the DTC (direct to consumer) advertising by pharmaceutical companies. First allowed in New Zealand, the practice then migrated to the U.S. TV ads give vivid descriptions of illnesses, for which one may require a drug that has side effects so extreme they could even be fatal. That is an obvious and blatant form of suggestion, and there are actions being proposed to curb the constant DTC advertising.

A subtler form of suggestion has taken place in subliminal advertising—something that is below the conscious recognition of an individual. A person may act on the unnoticed stimuli without realizing that he has been influenced to do so. Though there is no federal or state law in the U.S. to make the practice illegal, it has been taken up by various agencies, with the result that some companies and even networks have banned subliminal advertising.

There is an obvious need to protect and defend society, but for this next problem there are no laws in place, and no defense budget or recognized system of defense. It is the robbing of an individual's own free thought process. This was highlighted in my dad's experience when a prisoner of war on the island of Java during the Second World War.

In answer to prayer, he had received the message to "Control Thought." He knew the message meant his own, not someone else's, thinking. This had amazing results even to the point of saving his life. But there was one night he felt a mental intrusion was taking place, and that he had to stay awake and protect his thinking. He wrote about this in his book *The Ultimate Freedom*. "I had not been long enough in the Orient to become knowledgeable about the common practice of mental manipulation."

Though ignorant of what was taking place, he obeyed the intuition and was successful in defending his thinking from the mental invasion. He forgot all about it until towards the end of the war, when he met a Javanese man who claimed to know him. Here is the story.

> It seems he had been present the night when my captors had attempted to subject me to mental manipulation, or suggestion, for the purpose of questioning me. The reason he remembered me so well, he said, was that this attempt to manipulate me mentally had no effect on me whatever. He was so impressed by this that he had noted my name, rank and service number.

That a false influence has been used against the United States is being slowly recognized. There is concern this year that American elections are being influenced by hostile nations. Such dealings would be traceable at some point. But the pathway of unseen mental influences would not be so apparent. Let's return for a moment to the youth of the '60s and the war against parents, referred to as "The Saddest of all Wars" in the book *Quiet Answers*.

If a foreign power intended to destroy a nation's viability or ability to defend itself, a good target to influence would be the youth. To set the youth (the fighting force) against both parents and country would place that country in a vulnerable position. And though some of the causes of the '60s appeared to be worthy of advancing, the war on parents was totally unprovoked and unworthy. It caught fire and traveled from campus to campus in colleges and universities—institutions populated by the young. The anti-establishment revolt was carried out by students, who were being put through school by the very parents they were attacking.

Ironically, the parents were part of what has been called "The Greatest Generation" and the youth were not usually from dysfunctional homes but were from advantaged or modest loving households. There would be no reason for thousands of them to take up the slogan, "Don't trust anyone over thirty," to which many added the phrase, "especially your parents!"

The term "radicalization" comes to mind. Usually applied to violent means, the term does include the non-violent, and is defined by Wikipedia as a process.

> Radicalization is a process by which an individual, or group comes to adopt increasingly extreme political, social, or religious ideals and aspirations that reject or undermine the status quo or undermine contemporary ideas and expressions of the nation.

We might ask: What caused the process in the first place? Was it truly the desire for peace or the betterment of society? The war in Vietnam was not popular, so resistance to it was understandable. But the turning of youth against the country and against parents was without precedent. Why the extreme distrust of parents and authority in general? It was as though the youth had been mesmerized to view parents and country as "the enemy." That same type of mental extremity has appeared again today in this current era.

There have been powerful advocates for justice all throughout human history. They have fought passionately under the banner of mercy, justice and truth. But extremism appears under the banner of outraged indignation, super sensitivity and an enlarged, unbalanced sense of injustice.

It couldn't have been simply an ardent desire for social justice or even bad parenting that drove the youth to such extremes. Their actions and anger had all the earmarks of a mental influence that was directed towards them—a radicalizing influence sweeping over them. We might take into consideration the Eastern influence that was so prevalent in the 1960s, from martial arts to religion (transcendental meditation) and medicine (acupuncture).

Were all young people affected by the strange influence? No, that trend did not appear to touch those, who like myself, were young parents at the time. Even if taking college classes, we had a more stable base than did the unattached youth, who had no one else but themselves to consider.

The observations or points made here are not theoretical. I had firsthand knowledge and experience with the situation as bewildered and heartbroken parents, being threatened by their grown children, came to me for spiritual help. I also witnessed incredible incidents of threats and anger displayed by the troubled youth towards their families. There appeared to be no way of reasoning with the influenced ones.

Today there are elderly individuals from that era, who are still in a state of extreme sensitivity and are bitterly distrustful of government. With periodic outbursts of anger, they continue to blame one or both of their parents for all that went wrong in their lives. It could be said these unfortunate ones are still "under the influence."

Because she had discovered a metaphysical system of healing, Mary Baker Eddy was very aware of what thinking can do, for the better or for the worse. For that reason, it would be profitable for society to heed her findings.

Under the title "Ways that are Vain" (found in the compilation *First Church of Christ, Scientist and Miscellany*) she called mental manipulation by various names, such as animal magnetism, mesmerism, hypnotism and mental malpractice, according to the context.

She further stated that the victim of mental manipulation is tempted "into the committal of acts foreign to the natural inclinations." The victims of this crime, and it is a crime, suffer dire consequences unless they resist the false influence. Of those consequences, she wrote:

> The victims lose their individuality, and lend themselves as willing tools to carry out the designs of their worst enemies, even those who would induce their self-destruction.

She explained that this practice, ". . . fosters suspicious distrust where honor is due, fear where courage should be the strongest, reliance where there should be avoidance, a belief in safety where there is the most danger."

If we see signs today of normal allegiance to our country, our system of democracy, or even our press being eroded, we might want to consider that mental manipulation is at work. It's not so important to know where it is coming from as the fact that it is coming. Our defense is to recognize signs of the attack, and to repel it by choosing mental allegiance to what we know to be good and peace-promoting. More than keeping out negative thoughts and choosing positive ones, this entails the understanding of where true power lies.

In an address on the Fourth of July 1897, Mary Baker Eddy explained the power of right thinking.

> Christian Science classifies thought thus: Right thoughts are reality and power; wrong thoughts are unreality and powerless, possessing the nature of dreams. Good thoughts are potent; evil thoughts are impotent, and they should appear thus.

> Continuing this category, we learn that sick thoughts are unreality and weakness; while healthy thoughts are reality and strength. My proof of these novel propositions is demonstration, whereby any man can satisfy himself of their verity.

Those "novel propositions" of yesteryear are no longer considered so novel today. Such concepts are finding their way into the mainstream of humanity's upward path, showing they are provable and useful in every situation.

A posting on the *Business Insider* website, August 12, 2018 was by Brandon Webb and titled, "Here's the technique Navy Seals use to overcome fear and adversity."

A former Navy Seal, now an author and entrepreneur, Webb recounts some of his amazing experiences and makes the point that the battle with fear takes place in one's own mind. In one situation, he said that mastery of fear was the only weapon the Seals had. And it worked!

What an excellent statement of "Control Thought" this Navy Seal provided readers with when he wrote:

> Mastering fear is not about becoming physically stronger, or tougher, or more macho, or more aggressive, or more stoic, or more pumped up. It is about learning how to identify and change the conversation in your head.

In conclusion, he stated,

To me, that ability to self-monitor and change your interior dialogue is one of the most critical faculties that distinguishes a mature, adult human, someone capable of functioning fully in the world. It's what takes you from victim mentality to being proactive, from blaming others to taking ownership of your situation and taking positive steps to change it.

That is exactly what my dad did in the prisoner-of-war camp. About the message to "Control Thought" he wrote: "From that moment, fearful suggestions, resentful suggestions, hateful suggestions were barred from entering my consciousness." He changed his "interior dialogue" and the results were spectacular!

With so many crimes, from the setting of forest fires to school shootings, being identified as mental health issues, it's impossible to avoid the subject of thinking. What it is and what it does will hopefully be thoroughly investigated during this new era of further exploration into human and artificial intelligence.

From kindergarten to college, classes on the need to protect thought would be a great defense program for any country to undertake.

Furthermore, it's difficult to imagine exercising a more basic freedom than that of controlling and defending one's own thinking.

The Fifth Red Buoy

The New Era

The golden thread of goodness and compassion has been highlighted, for it runs through history and will surely continue to do so until permanently woven into the fabric of human lives and government. We can look for it again in this new era.

When is the next or new era taking place? Well, as the nurse said about the scientific era taking over from the medical, "It's already happening."

There was such an obvious correspondence of events between 2018 and 1968 that all the signs pointed to a new era taking place right now. It was apparent so early in the year that I began this book in April of 2018.

After writing *Three Gifts* in 2014, I had assumed that the scientific era with its many inventions would continue for possibly hundreds of years. It never occurred to me that the era which took hold in 1968 would last only fifty years before a new phase would take over. But the signs are unmistakable. Oh, it appears we are still in the scientific era (a religious era certainly has not appeared again), and so scientific invention will continue.

But if, and that's a big *if,* trends continue, then the new era would be a search for a better understanding of mentality, of the human mind, and it would again be a binary system, .

The three systems, taking turns at being dominant, have had a binary partner and also a way of being enacted. We could chart them this way:

The Era..........Accompanied by.....Enacted by
Religion.........Government...........church or state
Medicine ....The law...................doctors & lawyers
Science ....Economics..............scientists & economists

It's rather strange, but there they are—government, law and economics—all playing a part together. And I'm not sure why it is happening. No longer "seconds" in a subordinate position, the three are causing major disruptions, mostly centering around immigration and its accompanying identity and economic problems.

The government is embroiled in disputes over immigration, while lawmakers and the press have put on boxing gloves and are preparing to "duke it out." Even economics and compassion appear to be at odds with each other. Through all this chaos emerges the identity question.

So, the new era, the science of the mind, appears to be coupled with the question of identity in this way:

Science of the mind........Identity........science & religion

A compilation of "the seconds" with their individual issues, plus identity, would be something like this:

Government, immigration, identity
The law, the press, identity
Economics, compassion, identity

Just as an interesting note: In 1918, it was illegal to criticize the government during that time of war. In 1968, there was much criticism of the government over the Vietnam war. And in 2018, the government is criticizing itself—appears to be at war with itself.

As our earth capsule hurtles through space, the warning light to fasten our seat belts is on. We have encountered severe turbulence and need to rise above it. One way is to understand the issues, without getting caught up in them.

Government, immigration, identity

In so many parts of the world, there is a strong focus on identity, both individual and collective. Nations fear they might lose their identity to globalization, and at the same time they do wish to be part of the larger world community.

A good example would be the Saudis. *The Christian Science Monitor* reported the following on May 31, 2018.

> "Saudis don't want to lose their identity, but we want to be part of the global culture. We want to merge our culture with global identity," the crown prince, who effectively rules day to day, told The Atlantic in an interview.

The vote in Britain, called Brexit, separating them from the European community, was a call for national identity and sovereignty (control over borders and immigration). The nation never had totally joined that union, at least not in their monetary identity. While Europe was dealing in Euros, Britain was still handing out pounds and pence.

Donald Trump was elected President of the United States on the promise to "Make America Great Again," (with emphasis on borders and immigration) thus placing a national identity quite prominently in the top spot and helping to win the election.

I'm sure those well-versed in political science could provide a more-detailed and accurate overview of many countries, so I won't expand the discussion. But, it appears that all roads lead to the subject of identity.

If nations fear their identity is being compromised, let's consider for a moment the plight of children and adults, who feel they are in the wrong body, the wrong gender. This difficult, often heart-breaking, situation goes to support the concept that gender is mental, not material or physical. Identity has now entered the mental realm.

So, these national questions may arise: What is the identity of a nation? Is it confined to race, ethnicity and a culture that has been passed down for centuries? Could a nation's identity be not merely physical, but mental too?

America is a nation of immigrants without a common ethnicity. Fareed Zacharia said in one of his TV programs, "America was not founded on ethnicity, but on ideals." (Or words to that effect.) America's ideals are already set in place and can be found in the Declaration of Independence and in The Constitution of the United States. Oh, there may be a long way to go in proving equality and justice for all, but those are the goals and the ideals of this nation. They are bound up in its identity.

Britain's Magna Carta of human rights and liberty, written in 1215, provided a platform for humanity and other nations like the U.S. to stand upon. Though not explicitly stated, it also promised democracy. The British character is still imbued with those ideals.

As countries fear their national identity is being challenged by an influx of immigrants from many parts of the world, now is the perfect time to consider national identity in a different light. We can look beyond the material, physical race or ethnicity to the mental makeup of a nation.

The American character has been formed by the ideals of freedom, boundless opportunity, invention, innovation and a spirit of "can do." Though other countries possess a racial and ethnic identity, they also have a prevailing mental character formed by their ideals and values, and perhaps it is that identity which needs to come to the fore, in order for ethnicity to recede. For instance, Britain is known for its commitment to fair play whether in sports or a bus queue. The British possess integrity, a stalwart character, and a fortitude that endures hardships without complaint.

Such mental and moral qualities constitute the character or identity of a nation with which immigrants may unite, regardless of their own race or ethnicity. In this way, a nation cannot lose its own identity, if that identity is perceived to exist not solely on a physical basis, but on a mental and moral level as well.

The law, the press, identity

For a free society or nation to maintain its identity, it must support freedom of the press and of speech. Those lawmakers who sit in the seats of government usually have a reasonable, if sometimes adversarial, relationship with the press. Today that relationship has been severely strained, to say the least. The press is even being accused of disseminating "fake news."

Where has praise for dedicated, intrepid reporters gone? Not so long ago, Bob Woodward and Carl Bernstein achieved almost hero status by breaking the story on Watergate for the *Washington Post.* Those of us who remember that event have not become totally distrustful of the press, or at least the portion of it that attempts to retain high standards.

So, what is different this year of 2018? What thought trends have brought us to this point? It appears to be a twofold answer. One trend is found in the press itself, while the other resides in the readership.

Matt Bai is a journalist and political commentator for Yahoo News, and on July 26, 2018 his column was headed: "Plenty of presidents lie. Only Trump doesn't care if you catch him." Bai made the point that Nixon feared the consequences of truth coming to the surface, but that is not the case in this current administration. He wrote:

> To put it starkly, Trump is the first president in my lifetime to essentially say to the press that covers him: "Go ahead, jump up and down, prove all the lies you want with your fact

checks and your transcripts and your phony outrage. Nobody believes you anyway."

However, Bai next offers a blunt comment about his own field of journalism.

> Now, as I've written before, my industry bears a lot of the blame for making this possible. My colleagues in the media often seem to blame Trump for creating and stoking the public's abject distrust, when in fact it was our own vanity and triviality — the glib cable punditry, the obsession with rumors and ratings — that created *him*.

This honest admission makes the point that a push for ratings opens the door for untruths to enter in. The press, like politics, has had a checkered past. The infamous mud-slinging competition between the newspaper giants, Hearst and Pulitzer, to see who could dredge up the most sensational news, was known as a period of yellow journalism. Public figures, such as Mary Baker Eddy, were often targets in this ratings and revenue war. Seeing the need for honesty and truth telling, and at the advanced age of 87, this religious leader founded the *Christian Science Monitor* in 1908. The *Monitor* carries the motto, "To injure no man, but to bless all mankind."

According to its website, the *Christian Science Monitor* has won seven Pulitzer Prizes and countless awards in both the U.S. and overseas. The paper has been known for avoiding the type of sensationalism all too common in the field of journalism."

This newspaper was one of the few news sources allowed Nelson Mandela during his imprisonment of 27 years in South Africa over the apartheid struggle. The value of impartial, honest news was recognized even by those who imprisoned Mandela.

The press must carry the torch of truth and worthwhile fact reporting, or its image will be tarnished, even to the point of its news being deemed worthless.

But that is only one side of the coin. The other side pertains to the hunger for truth in the general populace. Just how hungry is society for the truth? A program on the company ILM (Industrial Light and Magic), formed by George Lucas in 1975, showed the amazing progress of visual effects in film. The use of morphing shapes, such as changing the face of one person into another in a single step, is becoming commonplace.

It seems that the desire for entertainment has overtaken the need for truth. In 1994, when the movie *Forrest Gump* blurred the line between fact and fiction by depicting Forrest shaking hands with President Kennedy, there were many concerns raised. Today that wouldn't create a stir. Like the morphing shapes, the lines between fact and fiction have become constantly blurred.

Do we care about what is real or true? There are reality shows that are not truly real, and the public knows it. This practice tends to numb one to the need for truth. Society's demand for truth-telling would do much in forwarding the cause of truth and in achieving better journalism.

When the vote for women was having such a difficult time being passed, Mary Baker Eddy made note of this in her book *Science and Health* in the chapter "Marriage." Under the paragraph heading, "Unfair discrimination" she explained the unfair differences between the rights of men and women. She stated her moderate hope that the amendment would be passed, if it did not incur further difficulties. Then she offered a viable solution to the problem through a pathway of improvement.

> A feasible as well as rational means of improvement at present is the elevation of society in general and the achievement of a nobler race for legislation, — a race having higher aims and motives.

Now, where does that leave the press? If the competing press were to abandon its ratings search and the promotion of sensational, trivial news, it could play a major role in achieving that "nobler race for legislation."

And if the press were to take up the identity issue, they might ask different questions of any prime minister, leader or president. For example: What do you consider to be the identity of this nation? Are your own ideals and values in agreement with the founding documents of the country? Do you intend to change the spirit or letter of the founding documents, or the identity of the country?

A note about founding documents might be helpful at this point. There is also an identity to writings and documents. They contain both the spirit in which they were written, including intent, and the letter, which is the content. Due to changing times, when the founding documents of a country, a church, or any organization seem out of date with the current era, what can be done? If the ideals are still valued and valuable, but if the letter is no longer applicable, then the spirit of those documents will certainly rise to our rescue and help clarify the meaning.

The Second Amendment (to the Constitution of The United States) regarding bearing arms would be a good example, as there no longer exists the type of militia to which it refers. The letter is out of date. Gaining the spirit and intent of that amendment should go a long way to stemming gun violence and protecting our schools and communities.

The high ideals and values set down in founding documents are only part of establishing an honest and honorable national identity. The other part is born as the citizens live and practice those ideals. It is that second part—the spirit which breathes life into the letter of the document—which forms an even higher national identity.

Economics, compassion, identity

The acceptance of a higher mental identity should help dispel the fear a country might entertain about losing its physical identity. But how can the refugee or immigration problem itself be solved? So many countries are being faced with this dilemma and there appears to be no easy answer. Nations keep searching for political and economic solutions, but there is one that never fails. Love always finds a way.

"Love wins" is the theme of the new and youngest Prime Minister of Ethiopia, Abiy Ahmed, a man with a Muslim father and a Christian mother.

Loving compassion for others had to be the impelling reason that Greece took in a disproportionate number of refugees in 2015 despite being in a financial crisis.

It's not always a country, but individuals who will reach out to help the displaced or abandoned. A woman named Wendy, whom I met in the late '90s was in her forties and had survived a difficult marriage. She was of Japanese descent and yearned to adopt a baby girl from China. Those abandoned baby girls were refugees due to a governmental system, not necessarily through choice of the mother.

Though now single, my friend bravely went forward on her mission to adopt. In preparation, she made a scrapbook for the new child and asked what I thought should be entered on the page describing the adoption. I suggested that she tell the baby she had been doubly loved, first by a birth mother, who had to give her up, and then by the new mother, who was waiting with open arms and heart full of love to receive her. The page was finally finished and spotted with tears but overflowing with love.

The beautiful ending to this story was that a friend of the new mother told a man she knew about the adoption and he wanted to meet that unselfish, loving woman. Long story short, they met and married. The new dad was of Chinese lineage, so the baby now had a Chinese surname. Nothing was lost in the transition. The racial, ethnic background was there, but only as a background, for the real story pivoted on one thing, on love alone!

Yes, Prime Minister Ahmed! Love wins!

Speaking of parental love, parents will love a child even to the point of sending it on a trek alone into a strange country, in the attempt to save its life. But this isn't new, is it? Moses' mother sent her baby floating down the river alone in a basket to save his life. He was found and raised by Pharaoh's daughter for, as the Bible records, "she had compassion on him, and said, this is one of the Hebrews' children." This incident, in the Book of Exodus, is the first mention of compassion in the Bible.

After revealing the Ten Commandments, Moses gave the instruction, "Also thou shalt not oppress a stranger: for ye know the heart of a stranger, seeing ye were strangers in the land of Egypt."

Much later in biblical history, Jesus' life was made safe when Mary and Joseph took him, as a newborn, into Egypt for refuge. History has acknowledged and recorded what those two refugees have accomplished.

The last biblical reference to compassion is in the Book of Jude with the counsel, "And of some have compassion, making a difference." The humaneness of humanity loves to make a difference!

When a fund was begun in 2018 on Facebook to aid the plight of immigrant children in the U.S., money poured in. The goal of raising $1,500 was far surpassed as the amount climbed to $15 million. There was no report of strained pocketbooks, as the donations flowed in from what seemed to be an unlimited source. Economics and compassion were totally in balance, and humanity's ledger sheet showed no shortfall or negative cash flow.

Portia in Shakespeare's *Merchant of Venice* could well be the reporter of this news, and she might comment in these famous words on the phenomenon:

> The quality of mercy is not strained.
> It droppeth as the gentle rain from heaven
> Upon the place beneath. It is twice blest:
> It blesseth him that gives and him that takes.

It would be fitting to include here part of the sonnet, "The New Colossus," written by the American poet Emma Lazarus in 1883 to raise money for a pedestal for the Statue of Liberty, which was a gift from France to America.

> "Keep, ancient lands, your storied pomp!" cries she
> With silent lips. "Give me your tired, your poor,
> Your huddled masses yearning to breathe free,
> The wretched refuse of your teeming shore.
> Send these, the homeless, tempest-tost to me,
> I lift my lamp beside the golden door!"

Once more, we have a woman with a lamp, tenderly epitomizing the light of love, and the welcoming spirit of the New Land. These concepts have formed America's ideals, which are not easily dismissed in the face of adversity, or when we find ourselves in difficult or seemingly impossible situations. This is no argument for thoughtless acceptance into this country, but for a wise love that seeks and finds the right way to live up to its ideals.

America has always been generous to friend and foe alike and was often first to stretch out a hand to its opponent and help raise a defeated nation back up on its feet. It has always given more than it has received, and therein lies its greatness and its genius. Generosity is an integral part of America's identity. The challenge will be to maintain that high altitude of thought during the turbulence of these times.

This whole section could well be summed up in the June 18th online *Christian Science Monitor*'s Daily Briefing by its editor Mark Sappenfield, as he wrote about the backlash against globalization.

> The underlying question to be answered is simple: Are we better off together, or not? The past 70 years offer a compelling answer. But they also suggest that, for the West, globalization is more than just cheap microwaves and lofty talk. It is a commitment to actually embrace the world.

The woman who was adopting a baby in China made loving preparations. Then she flew to China, with thousands of dollars strapped to her body, as the process demanded. She virtually "ran" across the world to greet and embrace her daughter.

There's another story of a parent running to meet a child. Jesus gave the parable of a prodigal son, who had wasted his inheritance in a "far country" and found himself destitute, desiring to come home even in the capacity of a servant. Seeing him afar off, the father in the story was filled with compassion and ran to meet him, prepared to welcome him as a son, not a servant.

Even in one's own country, it is possible to feel like an alien in a "far country," with hopes all spent—disappointed with life—a wanderer searching for refuge. Mary Baker Eddy addressed that human condition in a comforting message to her Church in 1902, when she wrote:

> Our heavenly Father never destined mortals who seek for a better country to wander on the shores of time disappointed travellers, tossed to and fro by adverse circumstances, inevitably subject to sin, disease, and death.

She went on to describe what is in store for those who make the spiritual journey, spiritual immigration, their goal. No identification papers or passport will be needed, for the warrant—the authorization to enter—is already there at the border waiting for the weary traveler.

> Divine Love waits and pleads to save mankind — and awaits with warrant and welcome, grace and glory, the earth-weary and heavy-laden who find and point the path to heaven.

This is a welcome awaiting each one of us! But, as we ponder that pathway, let's also look at the path "our big three" are taking. Let's consider science, medicine and lastly religion in the new era.

Science in the new era

The physical sciences have been branching out into life-changing areas in recent history. One branch is that of discovery and the other is invention.

Scientists have discovered matter's illusive nature due to quantum physics. Will they travel farther over matter's horizon into a wholly metaphysical concept, where matter does not exist at all?

Then on another branch of the sciences sits technology with amazing new inventions that are able to run on artificial intelligence. How far do we dare go in this direction?

Let's explore the inventive branch first. Science is taking an active part in pioneering the field of alternative energy. This activity will increase in the new era, as renewable fuel is needed, and transportation evolves. From the Model T Ford automobile bumping along on unpaved roads, we've witnessed rockets taking off for outer space. Now suddenly, pulling up beside us in a line of traffic, comes the driverless car. It's one item on the growing list of inventions using artificial intelligence and is subject to some human problems.

Google's driverless car, which debuted in 2015, was pulled over by the police for driving too slowly in its own hometown of Mountain View, California. It did have a passenger in the back seat, because at present the law does not allow it on the road without a human back-up.

As reported by *Fortune* magazine, "A car's legal driver doesn't always have to be human, according to U.S. vehicle safety regulators—it can also be artificial intelligence."

The U.S. Navy's first autonomous ship, "The Sea Hunter," is now being tested. This crewless ship uses radar, sonar and global positioning.

There is much experimentation and exploration taking place in the realm of mentality. Computers were programmed to do what thinking humans can do. "Machine learning," was an activity which grew out of the quest for artificial intelligence. This intelligence is now about to be enhanced by quantum computers. Here is an excerpt from an Internet blog on the subject published in October of 2014 under the title of "First demonstration of artificial intelligence on a quantum computer. The blog began with this statement.

> Physicists have long claimed that quantum computers have the potential to dramatically outperform the most powerful conventional processors. The secret sauce at work here is the strange quantum phenomenon of superposition, where a quantum object can exist in two states at the same time.

While we are still trying to wrap our heads around the idea that a quantum object can exist in two states at the same time, the blog goes on to tell of this remarkable feat:

> Today, Zhaokai Li and pals at the University of Science and Technology of China in Hefei demonstrate machine learning on a quantum computer for the first time.

111

> Their quantum computer can recognise
> handwritten characters, just as humans can
> do, in what Li and company are calling the
> first demonstration of "quantum artificial
> intelligence."

It goes without saying that quantum computing would drastically change the scene for artificial intelligence, and it may be a great benefit to society. But can this new frontier reach too far?

We may recall Steven Hawking's statement and concern for the future in that BBC interview in 2014, the same year as that blog from China was published. He said, "The primitive forms of artificial intelligence we already have, have proved very useful. But I think the development of full artificial intelligence could spell the end of the human race."

He probably wasn't talking about the autonomous car or ship, or even the cow-milking robots, that might help save dairy farms. It's difficult to know what he envisioned, but most of us can readily see that the integration of technology and electronics into the human body could create quite a problem. Yes, computers—common or quantum—being melded with the human body is a whole different matter!

When we consider that some companies are considering placing a microchip in their employees for identity and tracking purposes, it's obvious that electronics are entering the human body at an increasing rate. There is also speculation about changing a person's thought patterns through electronic means. If so, will the human race lose its identity? Will we lose the distinction between the human and the machine? Perhaps that was the question that troubled Hawking. Science fiction might become science fact. Cyborg existence could be approaching.

So, the question will not only be what identity is, but what reality is. And, in which direction will technology travel next?

Let's look now at the other branch of the sciences with their excursion, via quantum physics, into subatomic realms to find anything of substance in matter.

Dr. Milo Wolff, a mathematical physicist, summed up some thoughts on quantum physics and his own theory of a Space Resonance in these words:

> That is, all the matter in the Universe is made of waves in empty space and nothing more! All the "material" properties of matter and its "fields" are only schaumkommen (Schroedinger's words)—they're only appearances.

If matter's material properties are nothing more than "appearances," only waves, that's about as close to nothing one can get without crossing over the line into a totally mental or metaphysical universe.

I must admit that I had laid the concept of a man-centered universe at the feet of Max Planck due to his discovery of quantum mechanics. But when researching for this book, I found out facts to the contrary. It was evidently deductions made by others about his discovery that brought the man-centered theory into play. This proves how important it is to consult the founder of any science or religion and not be led astray by others' opinions. Here is what Planck said in a lecture on the relationship between religion and science.

> Religion and natural science are fighting a joint battle in an incessant, never relaxing crusade against scepticism and against dogmatism, against disbelief and against superstition, and the rallying cry in this crusade has always been, and always will be: *"On to God!"*

There is much evidence of that joint crusade of religion and natural science. According to Michio Katu, a theoretical physicist at City College, City University of New York, those in pursuit of a unified field theory seek "an equation an inch long that would allow us to read the mind of God."

Arno Penzias, the American physicist and Nobel laureate for the discovery of the cosmic background radiation which substantiated the Big Bang theory, stated:

> The best data we have are exactly what I would have predicted had I nothing to go on but the five books of Moses, the Psalms, the Bible as a whole, in that the universe appears to have order and purpose.

Albert Einstein developed the special and general theories of relativity and received a Nobel Prize for describing the law of photoelectric effect. Though he denied the inspiration of Scripture, yet his statements reveal an intuitive conviction that there is a higher, divine power and intelligence. He said:

> My religion consists of a humble admiration of the illimitable superior spirit who reveals himself in the slight details we are able to perceive with our frail and feeble minds. That deeply emotional conviction of the presence of a superior reasoning power, which is revealed in the incomprehensible universe, forms my idea of God.

Werhner von Braun, NASA engineer and scientist, and designer of the Saturn rockets, makes a strong case for the presence of God with this argument.

> I find it as difficult to understand a scientist who does not acknowledge the presence of a superior rationality behind the existence of the universe as it is to comprehend a theologian who would deny the advances of science. And there is certainly no scientific reason why God cannot retain the same relevance in our modern world that He held before we began probing His creation with telescope, cyclotron, and space vehicles.

And then we have Joel Primack, who is a Fellow of the American Physical Society, and a Professor of Physics at the

University of California, Santa Cruz. He studies dark matter, particle astrophysics, cosmology and quantum field theory.

> In the last few years astronomy has come together so that we're now able to tell a coherent story [of how the universe began]… This story does not contradict God, but instead enlarges [the idea of] God.

Sir Isaac Newton, perhaps the most renowned scientist of all time said, "All my discoveries were made in answer to prayer." Admitting his discovery of gravity came up short, this great thinker commented: "Gravity explains the motions of the planets, but it cannot explain who sets the planets in motion. God governs all things and knows all that is or can be done." Newton's direction was always Godward.

Now, what about quantum physics? Where will it tend? Perhaps this statement on homoeopathy from Mary Baker Eddy's *Miscellaneous Writings* gives us a clue.

> Homoeopathy is the last link in material medicine. The next step is Mind-medicine. Among the foremost virtues of homoeopathy is the exclusion of compounds from its pharmacy, and the attenuation of a drug up to the point of its disappearance as matter and its manifestation in effect as a thought, instead of a thing.

If quantum physics were to remove all traces of matter (including its ethereal form), so that matter becomes a thought only and not a thing, it might provide the "last link" in material science. The next step would be the Science of the divine Mind. Physics would not become metaphysics, but rather, metaphysics would take the place of physics.

If those in the field of physical science today would return to their roots—heed the words and ideals of their founding fathers, such as Newton, Planck and Einstein —they would surely be amazed. A new type of interest in Jesus might even emerge. He performed feats that defied the laws of physics when he walked on water, stilled the waves and was instantly at a destination. That names only a few of his scientific feats. How did he do it? That his spiritual, metaphysical Science was totally different from, and far beyond, any material, physical science, could be the only explanation.

The sciences, and especially quantum physics, are now at a most interesting place, even at a crossroads. Which direction will they take? If they continue to find no substance in matter, will that spur them on to explore a spiritual path? This new direction would be more exciting than any other they have pursued. At some future date, scientists may ponder that spiritual path in the light of the last verse of Robert Frost's poem, "The Road Not Taken."

> I shall be telling this with a sigh
> Somewhere ages and ages hence:
> Two roads diverged in a wood, and I—
> I took the one less traveled by,
> And that has made all the difference.

Speaking of the future, perhaps someone will establish a special chair in a university, as did the wealthy Englishman Thomas Hollis for Harvard. In 1721 he funded a chair, which is still in existence today, to teach the subject of Divinity.

Mary Baker Eddy foretold that the education of the future would be instruction in spiritual Science. The founders of the physical sciences would probably say an "Amen" to the proposal of a university chair in spiritual Science. After all, spirituality was where they came from, and scientific exploration was where they were headed. They held to a spiritual cause, but had not yet arrived at a spiritual effect from that cause.

So, the question remains: Which direction will science take in this new era? Will the sciences and religion join hands? That would certainly support Max Planck's declaration that religion and natural science are fighting a joint battle and that the rallying cry in this crusade has always been, and always will be: *On to God!"*

Medicine in the new era

Medicine does not appear to be poised at the threshold of discovering matter's absolute nothingness as does the scientific community, but it is at the point of recognizing, to a degree, that matter is subordinate to thinking. The following discussion will bring identity into the spotlight again.

In the many television and YouTube programs and conversations on the mind ("Mind over Medicine" and "Mind over Brain"), we find signs of an emerging era, where thinking itself will be the subject of scientific and medical exploration and where matter takes a back seat.

This current era is providing both a challenge and an opportunity for the medical community. Mental diseases of all types have arrived en masse, it seems. Oh, you'll be told that they were always present but just not diagnosed. However, many of us, who can remember events of fifty or sixty years ago, would be likely to disagree. The numerous cases of mental problems in the young, such as autism (often attached to males), in addition to bipolar states (attached to any age), were not even on our radar decades ago. I was in the work of spiritual healing from 1961 onwards and such types of cases were not prevalent at that time. Now the case books of doctors are full of them. But, this being the era of the science of the mind, the situation is understandable.

Here is an opportunity for the medical community to consider a more spiritual approach to the mental problems of society. They are already edging towards the boundaries of material medicine, so why not push the envelope a little further? Stupefying drugs are not the solution to a mental problem, but simply add to it with side effects. As we know, the opioid problem is needing to be tackled worldwide.

In what ways might medicine be approaching a more mind-oriented discussion of the human scene? Let's consider a couple of changes in the medical field.

In this scientific age, doctors are well able to diagnose and treat patients from great distances. They can even operate on them though countries apart. Startling isn't it! But it comes under the new science of robotics and is termed telemedicine and specifically telesurgery.

An advertisement for a phone company promises they can "bring" the doctor to the patient, who may be thousands of miles away. The doctor performs the needed surgery while watching a computer screen, and a robot at the other end copies their actions and performs the actual surgery on the patient. In other words, it is absent treatment. The physician is not present with the patient.

Mary Baker Eddy had just such a category for Mind-healing in which the practitioner could be any distance from the patient. This mental treatment was possible, not through robotics or electrical means, but because there is no limit to the divine Mind, which is accomplishing the healing work.

An explanation of that is in the chapter "Physiology" in *Science and Health*. When referring to Christian Science, not medical science, and under the heading of "Absent patients" she stated:

> Science can heal the sick, who are absent
> from their healers, as well as those present,
> since space is no obstacle to Mind.

Here, it should be noted that Christ Jesus accomplished such works at a distance. After speaking the word of healing, the report would come back that the patient was healed at the very time that Jesus spoke.

The next step after telesurgery would be to treat that patient mentally, as did Jesus, without the robotics. Human thought has allowed for an evolution in medicine, so why not also consider the spiritual and medical system Jesus employed? It was always successful!

That may seem too distant a possibility for right now, but there is another subject already touched on that firmly places our investigation into the mental realm.

An unmistakable sign of the new era, in which mind or mentality is predominant, is an ever-growing list of the near-death experiences (NDEs), which are often related by members of the medical profession. Here is the Wikipedia entry on one such experience.

> Eben Alexander III (born 1953) is an American neurosurgeon and the author of the book *Proof of Heaven: A Neurosurgeon's Journey into the Afterlife* (2012), in which he describes his 2008 near-death experience and asserts that science can and will determine that the brain does not create consciousness and that consciousness survives bodily death.

Not everyone sees the same phenomena of a bright light or a tunnel, but most do report the feeling of a love beyond compare—an unconditional, all-pervasive, pure love in which they were encased. Due to that sublime feeling, they are reluctant to return to this life, until encouraged to do so, often by those on "the other side."

This was the case with Anita Moorjani, who was in the last stages of cancer and thought to be totally beyond help. She wrote of this in her book *Dying to be Me*. Her recovery was so quick, after recognizing her problem had been a poor concept of herself, that she was up and about after only a few weeks. What really convinced her to return was when she glimpsed that heaven is a state and not a place.

She explains her experience in the context of her religious upbringing in the East. Others place theirs into their biblical background. This may account for the different "takes" on what happened. Not unlike the variety of opinions people hold about this life on earth, the conclusions and ideas about the next life also vary. For instance, Eban Alexander entertains ideas of reincarnation, while others do not.

The Baptist pastor Don Piper had recorded his meeting with loved ones after being killed in an auto accident. The film and book "90 Minutes in Heaven" tell the story. At the film's end, the actual pastor is seen speaking to a congregation and, at the time of that filming in 2004, he had spoken to 3,000 church congregations.

The various NDE stories support two important conclusions. Firstly, these experiences support the idea that the mind and brain are distinct. People can recount what takes place in a room, or even in the next room, while "brain-dead" and evidencing no vital signs. You will find many instances of this on YouTube.

There was one startling incident told in an interview with Dr. Lloyd Rudy, a pioneer of cardiac surgery, when a patient of his had been declared dead. He and his assistant, having tried every possible means to revive the patient, reluctantly removed their "scrubs" and were deep into conversation. One nurse came in and out placing stickers on the front of the computer with messages for the doctor. About twenty or more minutes later, there was sudden activity showing on the machines, which had not been detached from the patient. The person did revive and recounted all that he saw while "dead" including the placing of the post-it notes on the computer.

Science and Health contains the statement, "Remember brain is not mind." If consciousness can wander around apart from the body, then what is the individual's identity and where does it reside if not in the body? Could it be that the body exists in the mind and not vice versa?

Secondly, these many accounts support the conviction that there is life hereafter. Death is not fatal. Thinkers and writers throughout the ages have believed this to be true.

Helen Keller, who was the first deaf-blind person to earn a Bachelor of Arts degree, certainly had great insight. She wrote that "Death is no more than passing from one room into another."

Rossiter Worthington Raymond was an American mining engineer and legal scholar. He stated, "Life is eternal and love is immortal; And death is only a horizon, and a horizon is nothing save the limit of our sight."

Henry Valentine Miller, an American writer, went further in his description. "Of course, you don't die. Nobody dies. Death does not exist. You only reach a new level of vision, a new realm of consciousness, a new unknown world."

Mary Baker Eddy wrote: "Life is real and death is the illusion." She also encouraged humanity to act on this knowledge. "Life is eternal. We should find this out and begin the demonstration thereof."

The old taboo that near-death experiences should not be talked about, because one might be considered deranged, has been lifted. Doctors and nurses are well acquainted with instances of this nature, because their patients recount them and in detail. The medical system is being ushered, willingly or not, into an arena that was once populated solely by the religious—a belief in the afterlife. The Apostle Paul told the Corinthians that "The last enemy that shall be destroyed is death." A viable and current way to make a start on this is to stop believing in death. Wonderful results would follow such a step and, as announced by *Science and Health,* the standard of health and morals would be considerably elevated.

Though many doctors have acknowledged the often-amazing results from Christian Science treatment, there may not be the same general hunger or readiness for spiritual healing today as in the early days of Christian Science, when medical practices were so crude, and even life threatening.

Also, times would inevitably change. Being cognizant of that fact, Mary Baker Eddy wrote reassuringly that humanity's needs would always be met in any age.

> In different ages the divine idea assumes different forms, according to humanity's needs. In this age it assumes, more intelligently than ever before, the form of Christian healing. (*Miscellaneous Writings*)

Physical healing in Christian Science may no longer be the "bugle call," as Mary Baker Eddy called it in her era, but humanity does have an urgent need. It is to know that there is no death. The promise of eternal life in the Bible, as was preached in the religious era, is not as evident or heeded today, so the question comes up in non-religious ways.

Since about 2005, I've been contacted by people asking for *There is no death*—a book I don't carry. (The publisher's name is like my own company, and the book is about a near-death experience.) The prospect of scientifically knowing there is no death is a bugle call in this scientific age—a bright beacon, claiming mankind's attention.

One day, the biotech field will have replacement parts for the human body all lined up on a shelf, but there will still remain questions about effective healing, human and spiritual identity and especially life hereafter.

Yes, the identity question will surface again. What is the identity of the individual who has gone over that threshold, and through the change called death? Does it remain the same? It appears as if science, with the help of religion, may arrive at the answer sooner than the medical field, which is designed to repair the body rather than search for the individual's real or lasting identity.

So, what might the founding fathers of medicine have said about their field? My research found that there are so many branches of medicine, each with their own star, that it was difficult to select one. It was suggested, in answer to my computer question, that Sir William Osler, might come closest to being considered the father of modern medicine.

One can't help really liking this man, for he possessed the three great "h" qualities—humility, honesty and humor. Let's begin with this description from Wikipedia.

"Sir William Osler (1849-1919) a Canadian, was a highly respected physician, professor and writer who authored *The Principles and Practice of Medicine* in 1892, which served as the standard clinical medical text for 40 years."

Osler appeared to be right in line with quantum physics and Heisenberg's principle of uncertainty, when he stated:

"Medicine is a science of uncertainty and an art of probability."

Obviously, he had great respect for women:

"The trained nurse has become one of the great blessings of humanity, taking a place beside the physician and the priest, and not inferior to either in her mission." And then, "There are three classes of human beings: men, women and women physicians."

Here are some of his general statements about the art of medicine from the Internet:

"The person who takes medicine must recover twice, once from the disease and once from the medicine."

"Gentlemen, I have a confession to make. Half of what we have taught you is in error, and furthermore we cannot tell you which half it is."

"One of the first duties of the physician is to educate the masses not to take medicine."

"Soap and water and common sense are the best disinfectants."

The final two are very telling. Here, Osler highlights the mentality of the patient and its importance.

"Listen to your patient, he is telling you the diagnosis."

"It is much more important to know what sort of a patient has a disease than what sort of a disease a patient has.

Of course, much has changed in the field of medicine since Osler made those statements, but it's helpful to know his very honest view of medicine and its shortcomings.

Physicians are now becoming trendsetters by pressing forward to a newer, higher idea as medicine takes its place in this new more mental, scientific age. One thought trend is seen in the young woman doctor, Lissa Rankin, whose books and TV program focus on mind over brain. She said we had gone beyond simply mind over matter. Her book titled, "Mind over Medicine: Scientific proof you can heal yourself," was published in 2014. According to the Amazon description, "she explored peer-reviewed medical literature and found evidence that the medical establishment had been proving that the body can heal itself for over 50 years."

Mary Baker Eddy had referred to "the patient's spiritual power to resuscitate himself." This concept is more easily accepted today, as patients acknowledge they can take part in their own healing. Thought is constantly becoming more liberated, as old confining views of life are abandoned.

When the acknowledgment that there is no death permeates society, thinking will inevitably turn in spiritual directions. The possibility and advantages of spiritual healing will be viewed anew, and in a scientific context. For now, it is still a distant dot on medicine's horizon.

Religion in the new era

"The hour cometh and now is. . ."

Now is the perfect time for spiritual advancement and true worship. With church congregations diminishing, this current period might be viewed as a pause point for religion.

Whatever structures men may have fashioned in which to worship God, and no matter how dedicated an organization or denomination may be to its holy purpose, surely now is the moment for those human efforts to draw back in reverence and humility to allow the Word of God to take center stage.

John the Baptist knew he had to step back, so that Jesus might advance, for he said, "He must increase, but I must decrease." Jesus knew he had to leave, "for if I go not away, the Comforter will not come unto you." John's purpose or mission was "to prepare the way of the Lord," to set the stage on which Jesus would play his part.

If John hadn't decreased, Jesus would not have had full command of that stage. If Jesus had not left the human scene, after playing his appointed role, then the spiritual and scientific understanding of what he taught (termed the Comforter), could not have arrived with the discovery of Christian Science.

As an example, if a teacher in a mathematics class continued to show examples of his teaching, but never allowed the pupils the opportunity to do their own work, the students would never really understand what they had been taught. The willingness to step back and allow the next spiritual event to take place requires much humility and even great courage. In this new era, that appears to be the need once more.

If church organization is not willing to take at least a back seat to the Word, then the world may be deprived for some time of the glorious effects of God's Word understood and practiced. If it does step back to invest more deeply in the Word and gain a deeper sense of the Scriptures, there surely would be an unimaginable ripple effect across the world—one that might even approach the early days of Christianity, when the Gospel, the Good News, spread so quickly.

Science and medicine are increasingly placing thinking in a prominent position during this new era. Now, religion has the prospect of being a meaningful contributor to that conversation. It's an opportunity not to be missed! But religion, to participate in such a discussion, will also need to advance further into the arena of thinking and be ready and spiritually equipped to answer mankind's questions on the subject.

What does Christianity teach about thinking and its importance? To begin, we'll highlight the conversation Jesus had with the Samaritan woman in the Gospel of John. She asked about the place for worship. Should it be in the Samaritan's Chosen Place of Mt. Gerizim, or at Jerusalem where the Jews congregated? Jesus took her question completely out of the physical arena into the metaphysical—to a mental place.

> Jesus saith unto her, Woman, believe me, the hour cometh, when ye shall neither in this mountain, nor yet at Jerusalem, worship the Father.
>
> But the hour cometh, and now is, when the true worshippers shall worship the Father in spirit and in truth: for the Father seeketh such to worship him.
>
> God is a Spirit: and they that worship him must worship him in spirit and in truth.

And he often employs this type of "translation" method, out of the physical into the metaphysical, to illustrate his meaning. He changed the question "**Who** is my neighbor?" into the lesson of **how to be** a neighbor in the parable of the Good Samaritan. Obviously, Jesus used many figures of speech to advance his spiritual teachings, as his lessons were not focused on sheep, goats, pearls, or wasteful children.

Jesus taught by figures of speech common to his day, by metaphors, similitudes and parables, just as we would in our own times. The literal, physical meaning of the Bible has been a source of confusion to honest seekers for centuries.

For instance, there was a garbage dump outside of Jerusalem, which burned continually day and night. What a great example and metaphor for the inner anguish one would forever feel over wrongdoing, until it was repented of and made right. That would seem like burning in hell fire.

We might say to a tardy friend, "I've been waiting here in this restaurant for hours." Or how about, "I've told you that a thousand times!" They are just figures of speech.

The Bible uses numbers as teaching tools (seven for completeness, or forty for a period of trial). Jesus taught forever forgiveness ("seventy times seven") to his disciples. It would be a contradiction to believe that God would put His children into an eternal, fiery time-out for bad behavior. It just doesn't make sense, if we consider God to be unending Love. If we trust the Word, we must mistrust those human opinions which do not agree with the spirit of what is written.

Approaching our study of the Bible with those points in mind, we are far less likely to accept literal, physical interpretations, which lead to false doctrines and worship.

"The hour cometh and now is, when the true worshippers. . ."

What does it take to be a true worshipper? Certainly, those who are willing to investigate afresh the teachings of the Word would be on the track of Truth itself.

Our world today is riddled with rumors of fake news and countless contradictions. How refreshing it would be to invest in the Truth and find no contradictions in the teachings of Jesus. But, perhaps it is even more than that. To solve the mysteries surrounding Gospel teachings could well be the harbinger of things to come, such as spiritual solutions to the many problems and issues on the human scene.

Interestingly, it is a study of "the opposites," or terms and metaphors that Jesus used, which throws so much light on what might appear to be contradictions.

The opposites

The route I took to finding the opposites was through *Science and Health.* As a plan to research those concepts in the Bible, the following statement on page 99 stood out: Let's review all four of these opposing terms:

> The way through which immortality and life are learned is not ecclesiastical but Christian, not human but divine, not physical but metaphysical, not material but scientifically spiritual.

Not ecclesiastical but Christian

Jesus seemed to run up often against the ecclesiastical (pertaining to church government) way of doing things. The strict, literal interpretation of keeping the Sabbath was to do no kind of work, but his disciples plucked corn to eat on the Sabbath. Jesus healed the man with the withered hand on the Sabbath. A woman, so bent over she couldn't even stand upright, was in the synagogue one Sabbath when Jesus was preaching. He saw her, called her to him, and he healed her. When the ruler of the synagogue objected to the healing, Jesus rebuked him. (Luke 13)

> Thou hypocrite, doth not each one of you on
> the sabbath loose his ox or his ass from the
> stall, and lead him away to watering?"

And there was the incident of the woman caught in the act of adultery for which stoning was the punishment. Jesus wouldn't take issue with that cruel law, but instead suggested that anyone without sin should cast the first stone. They all left, so no one remained to accuse her, only her own conscience. It was obvious from Jesus' encounters that rigid ecclesiasticism was not promotive of true Christianity.

Through the years, church governments have been susceptible, as have secular governments, to abuses of power and privilege. The lesson we might take from this today is that church government is only as good as its ability to practice and promote a genuine and vital Christianity. If it doesn't, then church rules and procedures are meaningless.

Not human but divine

Jesus came to lead humanity out of the imprisoning beliefs of a world built on dust (matter). He had a dual appearing here. *Science and Health* explains it this way: "Jesus is the human man, and Christ is the divine idea; hence the duality of Jesus the Christ."

Jesus consistently chose the divine, not human, way. Notice how, in the preceding Bible quotation, he called the ruler of the synagogue a "hypocrite." A hypocritical human was far from expressing the Christ, the divine nature of a child of God. Jesus was able to rebuke the error of false identity, because the distinction to him was so great.

Humanity is suffering from a case of mistaken identity and is being penalized because of it. People believe they are mortals and sinners. It's kinder (though it may not seem so) to be willing to point out the false. Otherwise, the true answer may never come to light. A human being puts himself into a mental hell by indulging in states of thinking that are not in accord with divine Love. It is a human, material concept that errs and not the divine.

Again, Jesus insisted on the distinction between the human and the divine when he would not allow the man, searching for eternal life, to call him Good Master. "And he said unto him, Why callest thou me good? there is none good but one, that is, God." Jesus never said he was God. Instead, he placed himself with humanity at the feet of divinity by declaring, "I can of mine own self do nothing." The Christ he expressed was the divine nature, which had to take precedence over the human in every situation.

Not physical but metaphysical

Again, this is something that Jesus taught many times over. His emphasis was always on thinking, on mentality, so his parables and metaphors were metaphysical lessons.

The "wailing and gnashing of teeth" (Matthew 13), that takes place when we meet our Waterloo, is unavoidable. It is the battle to relinquish the material for the spiritual and the human for the divine, as when we are forced to give up the belief that our happiness and/or success depends upon a person, place or thing. Eventually all reliance needs to be on God, good.

Parables such as the wheat and the tares (Matthew 13) were lessons in thinking. What kind of thinking will we be accepting as our own? Are we willing to pull out and burn our own weeds of materialism, but not feel responsible for every wrong thought that comes our way? Sometimes, we may have invited wrong thoughts in, and at other times we have not. They just drifted in on the winds of general thought and attacked our own thinking ("an enemy hath done this").

And if there were to be no physical or favored place for worship, as Jesus told the Samaritan woman, it would logically follow there would be no physical heaven or hell either, but likewise states of thought.

One of the most emphatic statements, showing that Jesus was talking in metaphysical terms, is in Luke 17, when the Pharisees demanded to know when the Kingdom of God would come. How could one continue to believe that the Kingdom of God would be found in a special place or at a specific time after hearing Jesus' reply?

. . . he answered them and said, The kingdom
of God cometh not with observation:
Neither shall they say, Lo here! or, lo there!
for, behold, the kingdom of God is within
you.

In an address on the Fourth of July 1897, Mary Baker
Eddy repeated Jesus' statement in these words, which
removed heavenly good from a distant, physical future to a
present metaphysical possibility:

. . ."The kingdom of God cometh not
with observation" (with knowledge
obtained from the senses), but "the
kingdom of God is within you," —within
the present possibilities of mankind.

The tendency of human, material thinking is to place all
that matters into a physical location. So, there is a place
for rewards, called heaven, and conversely, a place for
punishment called hell. King David in his Psalms knew
better. He virtually declared that heaven and hell are states
of mind, and that God is ever-present, and a constant help no
matter what the human condition.

Whither shall I go from thy spirit? or
whither shall I flee from thy presence?
If I ascend up into heaven, thou art there: if I
make my bed in hell, behold, thou art there.

Not material but scientifically spiritual

Why scientifically spiritual? Perhaps, it is because "spiritual" could be simply an adjective, a general description. While "scientifically spiritual" carries a strong connotation of being demonstrable, or provable.

Jesus made clear distinctions between the spirit and the flesh, between a material and spiritual sense of life, when he said, "It is the spirit that quickeneth; the flesh profiteth nothing." Paul preached to the Galatians that the material and the spiritual are totally contradictory, "For the flesh lusteth against the Spirit, and the Spirit against the flesh."

We can't take a material body into a spiritual dimension. "Now this I say, brethren, that flesh and blood cannot inherit the kingdom of God," Paul told the Corinthians. We cannot experience the joy of spiritual existence while still holding onto material and fleshly beliefs about life and substance. It would be folly to invest in the fleshly human body or in any form of matter.

Jesus' parables showed the kingdom of heaven was like treasures found in a field or was like the pearl of great price, for which one would gladly give up everything. The counsel was to invest in the spiritual, not the material side of life . . . "lay up for yourselves treasures in heaven. . .for where your treasure is, there will your heart be also."

Jesus told the man asking about eternal life to sell all that he had and give to the poor. That admonition distressed the man considerably, for he was very rich. Material riches may buy a lasting name in history, but they cannot purchase immortality or eternal life. Only spiritual wealth can do that! And what is that spiritual wealth? Jesus explained it as a wealth of spiritual knowledge when he said, "And this is life eternal, that they might know thee the only true God, and Jesus Christ, whom thou hast sent." (John 17)

But spiritual, divine consciousness does not descend in one fell swoop and envelop material, human consciousness. It arrives by degree. We experience less of materiality in thought and in life and more spirituality as we progress. Christ Jesus described the way humanity takes in achieving the totally harmonious concept of life, termed the kingdom of heaven, with the parable about three measures of meal. This account is found in the Gospel of Matthew:

> The kingdom of heaven is like unto leaven, which a woman took, and hid in three measures of meal, till the whole was leavened.

Mary Baker Eddy likened the three measures of meal to three means of divine thought, which appear on the human scene as three modes of mortal thought. They are science, theology and medicine. We have been tracking the rising of those three measures, as they are being leavened. All three are tending to more ethereal, less material modes. A higher humanity is taking hold of human consciousness.

At the same time, human errors in thinking and acting are being exposed. When error or evil is brought to the surface, the ensuing turmoil is described by Mary Baker Eddy as a "moral chemicalization." She explained that God's law has uncovered the error or evil that Truth may annihilate it. It's a cleansing not a backwards process!

Facing faults

Jesus didn't pull any punches when it came to denouncing human errors of thought and action. He faced and exposed whatever was not in line with moral and spiritual law. He didn't fear the turmoil of the moral chemicalization that would follow such exposure. He didn't fear the displeasure of the individual or of the system. He was neither "politically correct" nor politically motivated. He was impelled by divine Love and empowered by divine Truth.

Obviously, Jesus would not be a good fit for our current society. He insisted on telling the human truth of a situation and didn't cover it up with good-sounding rhetoric or spiritual platitudes. People hesitate to point out someone's wrongs or faults, even in order to help them. *Science and Health* explains why that is:

> Because people like you better when you tell them their virtues than when you tell them their vices. It requires the spirit of our blessed Master to tell a man his faults, and so risk human displeasure for the sake of doing right and benefiting our race.

If society is not desiring truth on the human scene, how could it be prepared to receive the divine Truth that Jesus lived and imparted? Just think of what that one change would mean, if a nation's populace demanded truth be told! It would revolutionize all levels of government, and a great leavening would take place throughout our human systems.

Going forward!

The three measures of meal—science, theology and medicine—played a significant role in Jesus' own life. His mission involved all three of them. What he did with them, and the challenge he faced with each one, is discussed more fully in the book *Three Gifts*. We'll just touch lightly on each one, and also consider how Mary Baker Eddy leavened all three with the leaven of Christian Science.

The Lord's Prayer is at the heart of Jesus' theology. One could directly communicate with our Father, divine Mind, and expect to receive the needed answers. Likewise, Mary Baker Eddy proved prayer, based on the understanding of God's allness and power, is effective. In her Sermon, *The People's Idea of God*, she defined silent prayer and its basis: "Silent prayer is a desire, fervent, importunate: here metaphysics is seen to rise above physics, and rest all faith in Spirit. . . "

Jesus' medicine was of a spiritual and mental nature. He healed the blind, lame and sick with it. Christian Science treatment contains the same spiritual and mental medicine derived from the divine Mind. It has the power of spiritual facts that may be known and argued in favor of a patient, just as a lawyer would argue the truth in a courtroom.

An attorney either has a case thrown out of court (that's like instantaneous healing), or he argues the truthful (spiritual) facts for a client (the patient). While prayer directed to God may be given, without permission, on anyone's behalf, Christian Science treatment always needs to be at the request of the individual. The reason is: "When you enter mentally the personal precincts of human thought, you should know that the person with whom you hold communion desires it." (*Miscellaneous Writings*). The distinction between prayer and treatment in Christian Science becomes clear by studying the two chapters in *Science and Health*, "Prayer" and "Christian Science Practice."

Jesus' science was based on the evidence from his spiritual senses, and this enabled him to demonstrate power over matter. Students of Christian Science have followed his example in so many ways. Here is my own account which incorporates both Jesus' theology and science.

It was like standing on the edge of a deep, dark pit when Glen passed on. Trusting spiritual facts, not the evidence of the material senses, I knew that Glen was still going on living and working for God, and that I must do the same. But how? So, I asked God fervently, "What shall I do?" Immediately I heard the mental command, "Publish the book!" That was how I came to publish my dad's manuscript as *The Ultimate Freedom*. That single act of obedience changed my life and, according to letters received, the lives of so many others. Though the path has been somewhat rugged, requiring many sacrifices, I would do it all again!

Religious communities may feel they are facing an uncertain future, but bright new horizons and duties await them. Sincere prayers, without prejudice or self-will, do reveal needed answers. And just as in mathematics, the answer is there even before we ask the question. Jesus told us that! Those answers may not be the ones we want or expect but, when obeyed, they will bring amazing good into view. Lives will be changed, and humanity will rise higher.

The Sixth Red Buoy

Identity and Reality

Our own Identity

Shakespeare wrote, "To thine own self be true and it follows, as the night the day thou canst not then be false to any man." It's good advice not to deceive ourselves about anything, especially our own identity. But what is that identity? The times appear to be demanding an answer.

Identity is of intense interest to individuals as well as to nations in this year of 2018. Society is now in new territory and must solve many issues, including those relating to a transgender community. The great desire to have one's physical identity match one's mental identity is seen in the plight of even young children, who feel trapped in the wrong body—not their correct gender. They feel mentally out of sync with their physical bodies.

The transgender community is growing, which surely goes to support the concept that gender is mental. Identity is now firmly situated in the mental realm! *Science and Health* had placed it in that category over one hundred years ago with the statement, "Gender is mental, not material." But, the metaphysics of this subject will not be tackled here.

While gender is specific, there exists the general question of identity. It's not unusual today to hear, "We are spiritual beings having a human experience." That's hardly new, because in a Netflix series *The Pyramid Code*, this belief was also ascribed to the ancient Egyptians. The direction is radically different from the other age-old belief of human beings climbing up a ladder endeavoring to become spiritual. One is a top-down and the other is a bottom-up approach.

It appears that neither is quite the answer according to Jesus, though they both contain grains of truth. One concept begins with our spiritual identity and then lowers it, and the other suggests reaching for an identity that is not yet ours.

If we consider carefully the teachings of Jesus, we'll find that it's not a matter of our spiritual, divine identity becoming material and human, and therefore less of itself, so that we may learn life lessons. Nor is it a matter of a human being becoming something which it is not, namely a spiritual being. Rather, it is about being what, in truth, we already are.

In his Sermon on the Mount, when teaching the virtue of true impartial love—loving friend and foe alike—Jesus ended with a divine demand on his listeners. "Be ye therefore perfect, even as your Father which is in heaven in perfect." He acknowledged God as Spirit, so his concept of God's children would have to be spiritual too—as perfect as is the perfect Father.

Surely, he was telling us to be that which we truly are in divine fact—the spiritual children of the one perfect Father. It was not a become-what-you-are-not order. It wasn't a "become-what-you-used-to-be order, but "Be ye therefore perfect." It's as though he said: "Be the truth of yourselves and let the old concept die out."

When we think about it, how can we really worship God, who is Spirit, without knowing the truth that we are His spiritual children? If we know this fact and act on that knowledge, we will be worshipping Him "in spirit and in truth."

Of course, there was work implied in that demand, which agrees with Jesus' other command to "take up your cross and follow me." It means having to prove humanly a divine fact, even as one would with a mathematical problem where the answer is in the back of the book. We know the answer but need to prove that we understand the science of math enough to get there. A mathematical allegory may help at this point.

Numberland and identity

The book *Numberland* suddenly came to me right before Glen passed, and I put it down as it came, a chapter a day. It was published in 1995. (The book is now being used in Mexico, in a university class to teach English.) The book was followed soon after by a musical stage play, which had a short run, though the music CDs had a longer life. In 2017, it took the form of a Workshop/Musical titled, *Life Adds Up in Numberland: The Musical.*

Numberland tells the story of chalk numbers, who live on the Chalkboard in Chalkland. The characters, including a proud "perfect 10," attend a special school to find out what their real natures are like in *Numberland*. Yes, it is on the topic of identity!

Why is *Numberland* helpful? Due to its allegorical nature, it may be appreciated on a few levels. Firstly, it's just a good, often funny story about "numbers" (the odd numbers are male, and the evens are female) trying to solve their life problems. Next is the moral level to do with how the characters treat each other and finally the spiritual level of high ideals. And all action takes place under the perfect principle of numbers, to which they must conform.

The analogy has proved to be helpful on various occasions according to feedback from readers, and I too have often used it. For instance, when talking with two new acquaintances about life, I offered the following ideas: Our real, spiritual natures are like the invisible numbers, perfect and permanent. But the material, human experience is like chalk on the chalkboard, imperfect and erasable. They both exclaimed, "That's just what I think too!"

Now, let's take up those two theories again. The idea that we are spiritual beings having a human experience would be like saying the invisible numbers are having a chalk experience. That's not quite right, is it? The chalk is merely our own human, imperfect view of the real numbers.

The invisible numbers are not conscious of a chalk life, and the principle of mathematics could not be conscious of the mistakes that take place on the chalkboard. The prophet Habakkuk knew that about the nature of God. "Thou art of purer eyes than to behold evil, and canst not look on iniquity." God, our perfect divine Principle, doesn't know human mistakes and errors.

The second possibility of a human being trying to reach the altitude of spiritual being would be like saying the chalk numbers on the board are attempting to be the invisible numbers. They never can be that, because they are only chalk representatives, just symbols of an invisible mathematical world.

Orthodox theology has taught that the first perfect man in Genesis fell from grace due to disobedience and was banished from harmony and health. But using numbers again, we see that there is no "fallen man" due to sin or any other reason. An invisible, perfect number cannot fall out of Numberland onto the chalkboard. Those perfect numbers never made mistakes, and they never left Numberland.

The invisible, eternal life of numbers is taking place, even while the chalk erasable numbers are trying to work things out on the chalkboard of life. It appears that there is a quantum situation going on here, and that are two states of a number at the same time—the invisible idea and the visible chalk. But that's not quite it, either. Only one, the invisible, is the true state.

The first chapter of Genesis depicts the spiritual world and man's true identity. The second chapter is the mistaken view of life, the Chalkland scenario. That's the account of man's disobedience and his "chalk" temporary nature. The remainder of the Bible shows both the right and wrong way of working out the problem of the man made from dust.

Our human lives take place in our own thinking, and not "out there" somewhere. That's true of this world and the world to come. Only then, it will just be more obvious.

Hopefully, that example of the chalkboard will help as we consider some large questions about life, both before and after life on earth.

Identity before and after life on earth

To understand the reality of a perfect, spiritual preexistence will bring us into harmony and health. Mary Baker Eddy explained this in her *Miscellaneous Writings*.

> Mortals will lose their sense of mortality — disease, sickness, sin, and death— in the proportion that they gain the sense of man's spiritual preexistence as God's child; as the offspring of good, and not of God's opposite, — evil, or a fallen man.

And under the paragraph heading "Continuity of existence" in *Science and Health*, is this statement:

> If man did not exist before the material organization began, he could not exist after the body is disintegrated. If we live after death and are immortal, we must have lived before birth, for if Life ever had any beginning, it must also have an ending, even according to the calculations of natural science.

Our divine Principle, Life, has always existed, and its idea or reflection likewise has always existed. Before any life was apparent on earth this was true, and if life should disappear from earth, it would still be true.

The number, before it is written on the chalkboard, was always present in its invisible, perfect state. So, were we!

And though we appear to be limited, mortal, human beings (chalk on the board), the truth of us is right here to be discovered and lived. We lived in that perfect state before human birth. We continue to live it now, though chalk dust attempts to hide it, and we will continue to live it forever.

The supposition that life is material is all that is being proposed and that needs to be solved. This is the problem of being, which we will continue to work on hereafter.

Just as opinions are held about this object-oriented world, there will be opinions and conclusions drawn from people's experience in the hereafter, which appears to be more subject rather than object oriented. There are clues pointing in that direction. For instance, departed loved ones will often appear and welcome those leaving this world. It's as though time and space are eliminated for such a reunion. No one needs to go searching for that loved one, as they are simply right there. They exist as a subject in the departing one's mind and so can be seen immediately.

Some people reason that we need to be reincarnated and enter this same plane of existence again, so that we may learn all of life's lessons or to attain a certain state. That's like saying a youth, who has gone on to high school, needs to return to kindergarten to pick up what he missed or got wrong. More likely, he will need to take a remedial course and be put on probation for a time. Progress is required, not a return to old positions.

The problem with reincarnation is that it requires a belief in two things. One of those was brought up by a neighbor many years ago. He came to visit Glen and me with a specific question. "Do you believe in reincarnation?" But before we could answer, a strange look of recognition spread over his face, and he answered the question himself. "Of course, you don't! Because you don't believe in death!" He was right. To believe that one is born again into a material body requires the belief in death.

There is a second belief attached to reincarnation and that is the loss of identity and individuality, because one might return as a different person or even an animal. Mary Baker Eddy handled that under the heading, "One Cause and Effect" in her *Miscellaneous Writings*, when she wrote about Christian Science.

> It absolutely refutes the amalgamation, transmigration, absorption, or annihilation of individuality.
> God is the Life, or intelligence, which forms and preserves the individuality and identity of animals as well as of men.

This is fully in accord with what Jesus taught and did. Divine Principle, Love, gave him the power to raise himself from the tomb. He did not appear in a different form after what was considered death. It was the same identity he had previously. He even proved that to Thomas.

Nicodemus, a Pharisee and ruler of the Jews, came by night to question Jesus about the wonderful works he performed. Jesus told him of the need to be born again. It's obvious Nicodemus took that literally and physically because he asked if this meant another physical birth. The Gospel of John records the conversation.

> Jesus answered, Verily, verily, I say unto thee, Except a man be born of water and of the Spirit, he cannot enter into the kingdom of God.
>
> That which is born of the flesh is flesh; and that which is born of the Spirit is spirit.

Here Jesus makes it plain that one does not need to be born again into the flesh, or be reincarnated, to progress in spiritual understanding and demonstration. Water, often a symbol of purification, would indicate that purity of consciousness comes before one could accept Spirit, or the spiritual sense of identity and of creation. This act of being reborn, rising to and recognizing a higher spiritual identity, can begin to take place now in this sphere.

As identity is increasingly acknowledged as being on a mental not physical level, the next step will be to recognize that identity is spiritual. It is the reality that exists here and now. We will prove that reality, step by step, both here and hereafter until the clouds of misunderstanding melt away. We will be seen as the harmonious, immutable and eternal ideas or reflections of divine Love—the beloved sons and daughters of God.

Revealing reality

As mentioned previously, we create neither reality nor unreality. We simply come into accord with one or the other. One might make a mathematical mistake, but no one has created it. That mistake is just an erroneous supposition.

So, what is reality? The dictionary defines reality as that which exists in fact, rather than in the imagination, and as that which is immovable, permanent. This brings up the question: Can something that is changeable and temporary be considered truly real? If a doctor undertakes to cure a disease, he obviously does not consider that disease to be either fixed or permanent. In fact, he is doubting its validity or reality. One would never attempt to change reality.

There is a definition of reality in *Science and Health*, which is in accord with so many Bible references to the immutable, spiritual and divine nature of God.

"Reality is spiritual, harmonious, immutable, immortal, divine, eternal."

Therefore, we may reason that unreality is material, inharmonious, mutable, mortal, human, temporal.

These two sets of terms are used consistently as opposites in Mary Baker Eddy's writings. (Please do check that out!)

Under the reality definition, no one adjective is promoted or made of more importance than another. They are just different descriptions of reality.

Likewise, no one adjective describing unreality would be greater or less than another. They are all simply different descriptions of unreality. Let's see where this takes us.

Let's not confuse the human with the divine!

Surely, one of the greatest impediments to mankind's spiritual progress would be to confuse the human with the divine. (Human means pertaining to man, while divine pertains to God.) As we have just seen, the term "divine" is

150

part of the definition of reality and "human" is its opposite. In the same way, a temporal body or organization, existing in time, isn't eternal. These opposing concepts are found in the Bible and in the writings of Mary Baker Eddy.

As a start to clearing up any confusion between the human and the divine, we'll consider, in some depth, the question of Jesus' identity, which has been the cause of discussion ever since his arrival on earth. It was reported that he was the son of a virgin, a very spiritually-minded young girl named Mary, who had a vision that such an event would take place. That birth broke physical laws though it was totally in line with the law of the divine Mind, which doesn't require matter to propagate an idea.

Mary Baker Eddy spoke of Jesus' birth as that of a "human, material, mortal babe." (You'll notice that all three descriptions or adjectives are on the unreal side.) Coming in the flesh, Jesus was aware of unreality. However, he was endowed with the Christ, Truth, and so he also possessed the knowledge of reality.

In this dual appearance, it would seem to be a quantum situation again of an object existing in two different states at the same time. However, only one was the real, and the other—a human, material, mortal concept of that reality—would finally vanish. *Science and Health* describes the human Jesus and the eternal Christ this way:

> This dual personality of the unseen and the seen, the spiritual and material, the eternal Christ and the corporeal Jesus manifest in flesh, continued until the Master's ascension...

Though the real and unreal are two very different states of being, mankind is not without help in the matter. No one is left without a connection to the divine. There is a link! A wonderful point Mary Baker Eddy made in her book *Science and Health* was that Jesus' dual nature enabled him to be "that life-link forming the connection through which the real reaches the unreal, Soul rebukes sense, and Truth destroys error."

The "life-link" was like having a mediator in a difficult situation. This is one who understands both sides of an issue. Jesus was termed that by Timothy who wrote: "For there is one God, and one mediator between God and men, the man Christ Jesus." The difference between this and the usual sense of mediation is that God, the divine Principle, could not be asked to give up on a few points for the sake of agreement with the human. Rather, it's the human that needs to be reconciled to the divine. We don't ask the principle of math to have mercy on us and meet us halfway. To do that would be to adulterate and lose that unvarying mathematical principle.

The confusion between the human and the divine has plagued Christians from the very beginning. During Jesus' time there was much discussion of who he was. Matthew records that Jesus asked his disciples who they thought that he, the Son of man, was. (Notice that Jesus was referring to his human origin. So obviously, he was expecting a higher answer about his divine origin.) Peter didn't disappoint him. "Thou art the Christ, the Son of the living God." This answer was quickly approved by the Master.

Jesus was not an example of the divine having a human experience, but of the human coinciding or coming into agreement with the divine. He was perfectly reconciled to his divine Principle. One might describe it is as a chalk number that completely agrees with the principle of mathematics both in thought and in deed. Jesus made no mistakes or errors on the chalkboard of human life. He was sinless and came to show the Christ, the truth of spiritual being. That Christ, or divine Truth, has existed forever.

God had sent "his own Son in the likeness of sinful flesh," Paul told the Romans. The only limitation, or general sin, that could be attached to Jesus was that he appeared in the flesh. Paul promised the Hebrews that when Jesus reappeared it would be "without sin." Now, he had already told them that Jesus was "in all points tempted like as we are, yet without sin."

As Jesus was specifically sinless the first time here, it can only be concluded that the second time, he (the truth of man) will appear without that general sin of being in the flesh.

The Comforter, which Christ Jesus promised us, was not going to be a fleshy being, not chalk on the chalkboard. It is the divine Science, specifically known as Christian Science, which would reveal the real man as the spiritual idea of God.

Seemingly contradictory Bible passages can often be explained by the concepts of generic or specific, and the foregoing about sin and sinlessness is one of them. (A fuller discussion is in my book *The Golden Prayer Puzzle*.)

Christ Jesus taught humanity to look beyond itself, beyond the human to the divine, for help and healing. The prayer he gave us, the Lord's Prayer, is sufficient evidence of that fact. In addition, that prayer aligns us with the divine.

I had once wondered why Mary Baker Eddy ended her *Message to The Mother Church* in 1898 titled, *Christian Science versus Pantheism,* with the topic of "Prayer for Country and Church." But, it really was the perfect finish. It takes one beyond pantheism, or looking for God within man, to man reaching out to his divine source, the one Mind.

> Infinite Mind could not possibly create a remedy outside of itself, but erring, finite, human mind has an absolute need of something beyond itself for its redemption and healing. (*Science and Health*)

When Jesus said, "I am the way, the truth and the life. No man cometh unto the Father but by me," he was not referring to his human selfhood as "The Way" but to the Christ. The man Jesus was the human Way-Shower. The Christ, Truth, has always existed and will lead humanity out of its imprisoning beliefs of a fleshly, limited, mortal existence. But that does not take place without a struggle. The human concept fights for its own "chalk" nature.

If we believe that the physical body, which keeps on changing, is the real and permanent of us, then we need to think again, which is the meaning of repent. *Science and Health* states, "Man's individual life is infinitely above a bodily form of existence, and the human concept antagonizes the divine." Even Jesus had a struggle with the human concept:

> When the human element in him struggled with the divine, our great Teacher said: "Not my will, but Thine, be done!" — that is, Let not the flesh, but the Spirit, be represented in me. (*Science and Health*)

The Council of Nicaea in 325 A.D. grappled with the same question. Today religions are still attempting to meld the human and the divine into a singular creed in which they may believe. It is this area which causes the most difficulty, resulting in division and confusion in the ranks of sincere Christians. Students of Christian Science have likewise been put to the test on the subject.

Just as Jesus was inseparable from, but not synonymous with, the Christ, so Mary Baker Eddy was inseparable from her discovery of Christian Science but was not synonymous with it. (Synonymous means that one term or word is equivalent in meaning with another.) The ardent desire to accord the highest honor to any founder or leader could lead to the confusion of the human with the divine, bringing about schisms in a group or church. This has happened in ancient and modern history.

And should the confusion between the human and the divine enter spiritual teachings, it would adulterate them. In the early 1900s, the philosophical term "absolute and relative" became part of the vocabulary of many Christian Scientists. The phrase was used to denote absolute statements of Truth in comparison to variable human concepts, and it took the place of Mary Baker Eddy's distinction of the human and the divine. A philosophy doesn't heal and never claimed that it did, so a philosophical overlay would only prove a hindrance to the healing work so natural in Christian Science.

That mistake opened the door to the larger error of attempting to promote the human over the mortal, when they were both of equal standing on the unreality chart. Again, they were simply different descriptions of unreality.

Why was this mistake important? Mary Baker Eddy had warned "A single mistake in metaphysics, or in ethics, is more fatal than a mistake in physics." Another such warning is found in *Retrospection and Introspection*.

> Posterity will have the right to demand that Christian Science be stated and demonstrated in its godliness and grandeur, — that however little be taught or learned, that little shall be right. . . Unless this method be pursued, the Science of Christian healing will again be lost, and human suffering will increase.

"That little shall be right." To change the concepts or terminology of Christian Science, even slightly, would render it impractical and unprovable, just as it would in mathematics. The human tendency to make up one's own rules robs us, like those little foxes that spoil the vine, of the fruit of our labor—the ability to demonstrate divine Science in our daily lives. It's imperative that we trust the Discoverer and Founder of Christian Science by not extending her position or place beyond what she herself has stated. It's also necessary to adhere to her terminology and the spiritual concepts over which she labored for decades.

How important it is to trust Christ Jesus' understanding of his own place or position. He never did equate the human Jesus with God as we've already discussed, but this does not lower him in the eyes of Christian Scientists. In a letter To the Public" found in the compilation, *The First Church of Christ, Scientist and Miscellany*, Mary Baker Eddy made very clear the recognized place of Jesus.

> . . . all Christian Scientists deeply recognize the oneness of Jesus — that he stands alone in word and deed, the visible discoverer, founder, demonstrator, and great Teacher of Christianity, whose sandals none may unloose.

Does the idea of Jesus discovering Christianity startle you, as it did me? In reasoning it through, it becomes clear that Jesus arrived endowed with Christly understanding, but he had to discover how to put the Christ, Truth, into action on the human scene. That discovery was named Christianity. His process can be seen when twice he changed his mind about a course of action—at the wedding where he turned the water into wine (John 2), and when he first refused to heal a woman's daughter (Mark 7). His Sermon on the Mount is a wonderful explanation and teaching of Christianity at work.

Christ Jesus, as the Teacher of Christianity, infuriated the ecclesiastical powers of his day. In so doing, he laid all, even his own life, at the feet of everlasting Life and Love. And because he did, he could lose neither life nor love.

Jesus didn't destroy the reality of God's creating but only the human, mortal belief in something besides that reality. Sickness, sin and death with their material laws fell before Jesus' clear view of spiritual reality.

Let's now ponder the universe with its physical laws. Just how real is it?

Cracking the quantum code

The idea of cracking a code like that of The Enigma Machine, appeals to so many people, including me. I just love the idea of solving metaphysical mysteries that deeply affect our lives. The Bible itself appears to be a code book about life. Now, Newtonian, or classical physics, doesn't seem to present the mystery that quantum physics does, but it also needs a solution. So, let's see how the real and unreal definitions apply to the universe.

Is the universe on the spiritual or material side? The physical scientists have had a hard time finding any true substance in matter, so it's difficult to imagine that the universe, and man, reside there. Christ Jesus has told us, in so many ways, that God's universe including man is spiritual. Christian Science agrees with the Master Christian, as seen in this statement from *Science and Health:*

> The universe reflects and expresses the divine substance or Mind; therefore God is seen only in the spiritual universe and spiritual man, as the sun is seen in the ray of light which goes out from it.

If the spiritual universe is the reality, then our current material universe, though filled with grandeur and beauty, must fall into the category of unreality. This would seem almost too hard to bear were it not for the further explanation that the wonders of our universe are symbols of reality. If these symbols can be so magnificent, just think of how incredible the real must be! Therefore, even the unreal universe cannot be summarily dismissed with the wave of a hand. Comforting thoughts along that line are found in Mary Baker Eddy's *Miscellaneous Writings.*

> To take all earth's beauty into one gulp of vacuity and label beauty nothing, is ignorantly to caricature God's creation, which is unjust to human sense and to the divine realism. In our immature sense of spiritual things, let us say of the beauties of the sensuous universe: "I love your promise; and shall know, sometime, the spiritual reality and substance of form, light, and color, of what I now through you discern dimly; and knowing this, I shall be satisfied."

So, if this present world is not divinely real, then it is obviously in another category, which is again bravely and unequivocally stated in *Science and Health*:

> The visible universe and material man are the poor counterfeits of the invisible universe and spiritual man.

Now, the question must arise: What did the scientists truly discover in classical and quantum physics? It can only be answered that they discovered the sciences of a counterfeit world. Therefore, their sciences are likewise counterfeit.

But wait! We can't dismiss the sciences with a wave of the hand either, because they do provide clues, or symbols, relating to the divine Science that must govern the universe. When Newton discovered laws of motion and of gravity, he knew he hadn't really plumbed the depths—the description of the power that lay behind those laws.

We could liken Newton's situation to a mathematician who has discovered marvelous facts and rules to do with numbers on the chalkboard and who realizes those rules must have come from the principle or science of mathematics, though he cannot explain it. However, a mathematician who understood the science of numbers could. He would know why the principle that governs the invisible numbers must also apply to and govern the numbers on the chalkboard.

Christ Jesus, the ultimate scientist, did explain it when he prayed, "Thy will be done on earth as it is in heaven." *Science and Health* provides the spiritual sense of his petition: "Enable us to know, as in heaven, so on earth God is omnipotent, supreme." God's divine Science is found governing even the human scene (the human chalkboard), when we understand and apply it.

In the chapter Genesis in *Science and Health,* there are descriptions of the spiritual creation, seen in the first chapter of Genesis, and then of the material counterfeit creation, found in the second chapter.

Explaining the symbols in Genesis 1:10 of the Earth and Seas, Mary Baker Eddy wrote: "In metaphor, the *dry land* illustrates the absolute formations instituted by Mind, while water symbolizes the elements of Mind."

Here is where the physical sciences, in an attempt to explain a physical universe, depart from the main first cause—the immortal, divine Mind—by placing cause and effect in the hands of matter and a mortal, human mind.

"The absolute formations instituted by Mind" are humanly translated as a solid, material earth (including celestial bodies). The "elements of Mind" are exchanged for mortal mind's own elementary building tools (its own limited, false thoughts). This would be like a counterfeiter using the wrong ink for his fake bills.

By using the elements of mortal mind in place of the "elements of Mind," the counterfeiter has made some serious mistakes—flaws that are apparent to someone who is familiar with the real thing. The most obvious is the chaotic nature of quantum physics. There is no randomness or unpredictability in Mind's stable universe.

But not to worry! By noting this falsity, by seeing its counterfeit chaotic nature, we can put this fake and its random effects out of circulation by becoming increasingly more familiar with the real universe. In her book *Unity of Good,* Mary Baker Eddy wrote: "The chaos of mortal mind is made the stepping-stone to the cosmos of immortal Mind." The cosmos, according to the dictionary, means an orderly, harmonious, systematic universe.

It appears to me now (and this is only my current sense of it, for you will need to put all the pieces of this puzzle together for yourself), that quantum physics reveals the elementary, unstable building blocks of the human, mortal mind, while Newtonian physics takes into account the more "solid" and "dependable" appearance of a material universe.

In other words, the physical sciences deal with the human mind and its material manifestations and not with the divine Mind and its spiritual manifestations. As quoted previously, Mary Baker Eddy prophesied: "The education of the future will be instruction, in spiritual Science, against the material symbolic counterfeit sciences." (*Miscellaneous Writings*)

From all this comes the realization of how important it is to have a spiritual Science to explain the spiritual universe and to help us deal with the counterfeit.

But there is more to life than dealing with a counterfeit. There is scientific work to be done by all of us. Just as we would translate our language for a visitor from a foreign land, eventually we must translate all that we see of this material, limited, chalk world, including us. *Science and Health* says of material appearances:

> . . . they all must give place to the spiritual fact by the translation of man and the universe back into Spirit. In proportion as this is done, man and the universe will be found harmonious and eternal.

We can take small steps. Every time we experience healing in Christian Science of sin or sickness, translation has taken place. We can also begin by translating some of our human practices and institutions.

Translating politics

On October 8, 2018, the final question on the TV show Jeopardy was: Of the 23 statues of lawgivers in the U.S. Capitol, only one is from the Bible. The answer was Moses. The question was well timed, for the country had just undergone the most contentious nomination for a Supreme Court Justice in its history. Partisan politics and women's rights were all in the mix as demonstrators gathered.

When asked for the great commandment in the law, Jesus gave a wonderful summary of Moses' Ten Commandments. He replied the first and greatest commandment was to love God with all the heart, soul and mind. And the second—to love your neighbor as yourself—was just like the first. He made it very clear that both were required!

In translating politics back into a more spiritual sense, we may find that the main two political parties are a dim reflection of the two commandments—a human attempt to pattern the divine. The conservatives' concern with fiscal responsibility and streamlining government is held up as a good principle. The liberals' compassion for others—the desire to aid their neighbors—is just as necessary and makes for a balance. There is no room for partisan politics, because we cannot divorce our highest sense of what is right and good from love for our neighbor. They work as a unit!

Abraham Lincoln's stated primary objective was to preserve the Union. Continuing to allow politics to divide our highest and best aims into two opposing camps undermines the unity of "One nation under God, indivisible . . ." This is a serious and present challenge to the United States!

Challenges and progress

The challenge to our own individual progress is the temptation to consult others for spiritual inspiration and understanding. We can trust the Word of God, with its Christly message to humanity, to reveal to us what we need to know. Running to others for enlightenment and choosing to believe their opinions, instead of going to the textbooks (the Bible and *Science and Health*), constitutes choosing the human over the divine, and opens one up to mistakes and confusion. Individual obedience, not consensus, is needed.

The challenge to the Bible's instructions, especially Jesus' teachings, is that they are being side-lined and made impractical by literal, physical interpretations. If their spiritual, metaphysical meanings were to be accepted and practiced by Christendom, a tsunami of harmony, health and goodness would surely sweep over and cover the earth.

The present challenge to the Science of Christianity is that its message will be permanently adulterated by human opinions, and the Science be made of little effect. Only living the spirit of Christian Science, then understanding and abiding by its letter, will prove its efficacy.

It will take unselfed love and an abundance of humility to allow for the spiritual and scientific meaning of the Bible, the Word of God, to come to the fore. It will require those same qualities to relinquish false concepts about the Science of Christianity. Great courage is needed to rectify the mistakes of the past, in order to clear the path for the future.

Humility, love and courage! They changed the world two thousand years ago, and they surely will again.

Conclusion

Sitting in the blue boat

When our family left Australia, we stopped over in Honolulu for a week, so my dad could film the trip for the airline we were traveling on.

All went well except for one day when clouds and a light drizzle cast a shadow over the many tourists assembled at a picturesque spot for their photo-taking opportunities. One man was deeply disappointed that he wouldn't be able to capture the beautiful sun-drenched Hawaiian scenery on film. My dad, noting his dismay, offered the comforting remark, "Never mind, we're all in the same boat." The stranger, not being familiar with English colloquialisms replied, "Oh no, I came by plane!"

No matter how we arrived at this point, we are all sitting in the blue boat together perusing the past and pondering our future. The timelines have told their own story and needed little explanation from me.

The new era is in progress now with its pivotal year being 2018, and this new phase appears to be still under the heading of science. There will be more scientific investigation into the areas of mentality and intelligence (human and artificial) than ever before. So, at this point it still seems reasonable to call this the science-of-the-mind era.

Perhaps, the era's true designation remains to be seen or verified, but it does appear obvious that the era is accompanied by the quest for an understood and strong identity, both individual and collective.

After reading *Three Gifts*, someone asked if the eras would rotate again with a new religious era appearing. That's quite a question, and I must admit that thought is not really appealing. It was even suggested that Islam could be the next dominating force. That seemed like a very distant possibility, and I tended to dismiss it.

However, when 2018 signaled the change of era, the projections for the future of religion suddenly took on new importance. One Pew Research study predicted that, if the current trend continues, by the year 2050 the number of adherents of Islam will have drawn even with Christianity, and by 2070 Islam would surpass Christianity. Well, we can be a little more precise about that now, can't we! If the pattern continues, the year would be 2068.

How not to let that happen and why? Pursuing the why first, we learn from history again. When religion dominates (whichever religion it may be), exclusivity and control take over. Freedom of speech and the press is curtailed. Nothing seems to quite fire up and feed extremes as religious beliefs. Galileo is a good example of that. When his scientific work ran counter to the religious teachings of his time—he believed the sun not the earth to be the center of our system—the Church persecuted him. He was forced to recant and was put under house arrest for the remainder of his life. The terrible inquisitions also took place during this time. Though the predominant religion was Christianity, with teachings of peace, goodwill and love, extreme elements demanded their own opposite interpretation of Scripture.

One possible way to deter extreme religious elements would be to place emphasis on the golden thread running throughout humanity's history. We can give our attention to the areas we've pinpointed. A forward march to further equalize the sexes, protect the youth and support everyone's human and civil rights would take us farther up that mountain of progress we are climbing. A lived Christianity should ensure that religious domination was a thing of the past and not of our future.

There was no exclusivity in Jesus' teachings. When the disciple John forbade a man to perform good works in Jesus' name, without being part of their group, Jesus strongly replied, "Forbid him not: for he that is not against us is for us." What an amazing definition of "for" and "against!" There are no factions or cliques in true Christianity, as no one is forbidden to join the rising tide of impartial love and kindness that Jesus taught. Membership in that loving society is free to all who wish it.

Christlike love and goodness are a way of life, and Jesus was the Way-shower who taught by example. There are those who would never claim the label of Christian and yet are more Christian in their thoughts and deeds than many who do, so the title alone cannot be the determiner. And others, who have absolutely no knowledge of Jesus or Christianity, might be walking in that path or looking for it.

"The Gospel According to You" is a beautiful anonymous poem that has been around for some time. This is the last verse of the poem.

You are writing each day a letter to men
Take care that the writing is true;
'Tis the only gospel that some men will read,
That gospel according to you.

Love is the solution. The way we live our lives each day tells this love story, this good news, to others. There are many such love stories being told to humanity today.

James and Deborah Fallows share a story of hope and progress in their new book *Our Towns*. After a five-year journey covering 100,000 miles in a small plane, with stops along the way to interview people, the couple has compiled a record of meaningful interactions that points us in the direction of grass-roots goodness. Their description of how American cities and towns are reinventing themselves paints a picture of lively thought trends rising higher and higher.

In July of 2018, the Wild Boars soccer team of twelve boys and their young coach made their way, with the aid of many volunteers, out of a flooded cave in Thailand. They were all rescued much to the joy of the waiting world.

Teams from the United Kingdom, China, the United States, Australia and Japan were on hand to give assistance to the expert Navy Seal Thai team. There was no mention of possible trade wars with China and certainly no discussion of national identity. They were all of one race, one identity—a humane human race. Yahoo news reported that "millions breathed a global sigh of relief" when the ordeal was over.

Thailand's Ambassador to the United Nations in New York, Vitavas Srivihok, made a point of how many experts came to Thailand's aid from other nations.

> On behalf of the Royal Thai Government and the Thai people, we would like to express our sincere appreciation and deepest gratitude to all our friends from around the world who have offered a helping hand, with absolutely no discrimination with regard to race, age, gender, or status.

Surely, the journey out of that flooded cave is signaling to us in 2018, when we seem to be drowning in floods of partisan rhetoric, that we will emerge from that dark cave of division with the help of a team of angel thoughts guiding us. A higher humanity keeps surfacing regularly, even if it does gasp for air now and then. It simply can't be kept down!

A new kind of globalization has been quietly at work for many years now, though it hasn't been called by that name. In 2010, thirty-three miners were trapped in a mine for over two months in Chile and the world rushed to their rescue. Even NASA helped. It was reported that a billion people watched the TV news as they emerged from the mine, and what rejoicing there was! This is a globalization that everyone welcomes and appreciates. Perhaps the best term for globalization is collaboration!

When I began this book in April of 2018, the title came quickly and the cover too, so I wrote to that title. While watching the live streaming of a church annual meeting just two months later in June, I was surprised and delighted to hear this question being asked: "Where do you feel we'll be going from here?" So many listening church members all around the world were surely wondering that too.

The answer was just perfect. "Well, that is something that we will all have to discover together." This was no "top-down" type of answer. It didn't tell the members what was going to happen, or what they should be doing. And it wasn't a "bottom-up" suggestion of "you tell us where we will go." It was a totally collaborative reply, promising unity of thought and effort.

Many nationalities have compatibly manned the orbiting space station without any hint of animosity. They performed experiments and fact-finding missions together and freely shared the results. Our space capsule, called Earth, provides the same opportunity for friendly collaboration. Though our world may wobble on its axis of love that Jesus established, yet it is still spinning. Love is still the major driving force.

However, a question will inevitably surface, and I know because I've asked it. What if we do attain a higher humanity and a loving community, country or world? Might that not simply mean human goodness with no acknowledged connection to the divine? Wouldn't God, the divine Principle of our lives, go unrecognized in that scenario?

There's a reassuring answer to this question from Mary Baker Eddy in *Science and Health*. "The cement of a higher humanity will unite all interests in the one divinity."

In that same book is a description of the wonderful results of having just "one divinity." Our blue boat has been silently sailing, while we were contemplating the future. It must be nearing land, because we can see in the distance what happens to the many issues—immigration, government, globalization, youth, women, civil and human rights—that have been tackled, while we were traveling from era to era.

One infinite God, good, unifies men and nations; constitutes the brotherhood of man; ends wars; fulfils the Scripture, "Love thy neighbor as thyself;" annihilates pagan and Christian idolatry, — whatever is wrong in social, civil, criminal, political, and religious codes; equalizes the sexes; annuls the curse on man, and leaves nothing that can sin, suffer, be punished or destroyed.

Now, that is a destination worth sailing towards!

28784326R00096

Made in the USA
Columbia, SC
26 October 2018